THE ART OF WAR

THE ART OF WAR

AN ILLUSTRATED EDITION

SUN TZU

TRANSLATED BY
THOMAS CLEARY

SHAMBHALA
BOSTON & LONDON
2004

Shambhala Publications, Inc.
Horticultural Hall
300 Massachusetts Avenue
Boston, MA 02115
www.shambhala.com

9 8 7 6 5 4 3 2 1

First Paperback Edition

Printed in Singapore

⊛ This edition is printed on acid-free paper that meets the American National Standards Institute z39.48 Standard.

Distributed in the United States by Random House, Inc.,
and in Canada by Random House of Canada Ltd

Art Research: Donald Dinwiddie
Designer: Dede Cummings
Cover Calligrapher: Lee T'ing-Rong

Library of Congress Cataloging-in-Publication Data
Sunzi, 6TH CENT. B.C.
[Sunzi bing fa. English]
The art of war: an illustrated edition/Sun Tzu; translated by Thomas Cleary.
p.   cm.
Rev. ed. of: The illustrated art of war. 1st ed. 1998.
ISBN 1-59030-185-4 (pbk.: alk. paper)
1. Military art and science—China—Early works to 1800.   2. Strategy—Early works to 1800.   3. Leadership—Early works to 1800.   ¾. Cleary, Thomas F., 1949– .   II. Title.
U101.S9513 2004
355.02—dc22
2004010456

CONTENTS

Translator's Preface 7

Translator's Introduction 9

1.	STRATEGIC ASSESSMENTS	59
2.	DOING BATTLE	77
3.	PLANNING A SIEGE	89
4.	FORMATION	111
5.	FORCE	123
6.	EMPTINESS AND FULLNESS	133
7.	ARMED STRUGGLE	149
8.	ADAPTATIONS	163
9.	MANEUVERING ARMIES	171
10.	TERRAIN	187
11.	NINE GROUNDS	195
12.	FIRE ATTACK	213
13.	ON THE USE OF SPIES	219

Credits 224

TRANSLATOR'S PREFACE

THE ART OF WAR (*Sunzi bingfa / Sun-tzu ping-fa*), compiled well over two thousand years ago by a mysterious Chinese warrior-philosopher, is still perhaps the most prestigious and influential book of strategy in the world today, as eagerly studied in Asia by modern politicians and executives as it has been by military leaders and strategists for the last two millennia and more.

In Japan, which was transformed directly from a feudal culture into a corporate culture virtually overnight, contemporary students of *The Art of War* have applied the strategy of this ancient classic to modern politics and business with similar alacrity. Indeed, some see in the successes of postwar Japan an illustration of Sun Tzu's dictum of the classic, "To win without fighting is best."

As a study of the anatomy of organizations in conflict, *The Art of War* applies to competition and conflict in general, on every level from the interpersonal to the international. Its aim is invincibility, victory without battle, and unassailable strength through understanding of the physics, politics, and psychology of conflict.

This translation of *The Art of War* presents the classic from the point of view of its background in the great spiritual tradition of Taoism, the origin not only of psychology but also of science and technology in East Asia, and the source of the insights into human nature that underlie this most revered of handbooks for success.

In my opinion, the importance of understanding the Taoist element of *The Art of War* can hardly be exaggerated. Not only is this classic of strategy permeated with the ideas of great Taoist works such as the *I Ching* (*The Book of Changes*) and the *Tao-te Ching* (*The Way and Its Power*), but it reveals the fundamentals of Taoism as the ultimate source of all the traditional Chinese martial arts. Furthermore, while *The Art of War* is unmatched in its presentation of principle, the keys to the deepest levels of practice of its strategy depend on the psychological development in which Taoism specializes.

The enhanced personal power traditionally associated with application of Taoist mental technology is in itself a part of the collective power associated with application of the understanding of mass psychology taught in *The Art of War*. What is perhaps most characteristically Taoist about *The Art of War* in such a way as to recommend itself to the modern day is the manner in which power is continually tempered by a profound undercurrent of humanism.

Throughout Chinese history, Taoism has been a moderating force in the fluctuating currents of human thought and action. Teaching that life is a complex of interacting forces, Taoism has fostered both material and mental progress, both technological development and awareness of the potential dangers of that very development, always striving to encourage balance between the material and spiritual sides of humankind. Similarly, in politics Taoism has stood on the side of both rulers and ruled, has set kingdoms up and has torn kingdoms down, according to the needs of the time. As a classic of Taoist thought, *The Art of War* is thus a book not only of war but also of peace, above all a tool for understanding the very roots of conflict and resolution.

TRANSLATOR'S INTRODUCTION

TAOISM AND THE ART OF WAR

ACCORDING TO AN OLD STORY, a lord of ancient China once asked his physician, a member of a family of healers, which of them was the most skilled in the art.

The physician, whose reputation was such that his name became synonymous with medical science in China, replied, "My eldest brother sees the spirit of sickness and removes it before it takes shape, so his name does not get out of the house.

"My elder brother cures sickness when it is still extremely minute, so his name does not get out of the neighborhood.

"As for me, I puncture veins, prescribe potions, and massage skin, so from time to time my name gets out and is heard among the lords."

Among the tales of ancient China, none captures more beautifully than this the essence of *The Art of War*, the premiere classic of the science of strategy in conflict. A Ming dynasty critic writes of this little tale of the physician: "What is essential for leaders, generals, and ministers in running countries and governing armies is no more than this."

The healing arts and the martial arts may be a world apart in ordinary usage, but they are parallel in several senses: in recognizing, as the story says, that the less needed the better; in the sense that both involve strategy in dealing with disharmony; and in the sense that in both knowledge of the problem is key to the solution.

As in the story of the ancient healers, in Sun Tzu's philosophy the peak efficiency of knowledge and strategy is to make conflict altogether unnecessary: "To overcome others' armies without fighting is the best of skills." And like the story of the healers, Sun Tzu explains there are all grades of martial arts: The superior militarist foils enemies' plots; next best is to ruin their alliances; next after that is to attack their armed forces; worst is to besiege their cities.*

Just as the eldest brother in the story was unknown because of his acumen and the middle brother was hardly known because of his alacrity, Sun Tzu also affirms that in ancient times those known as skilled warriors won when victory was still easy, so the victories of skilled warriors were not known for cunning or rewarded for bravery.

This ideal strategy whereby one could win without fighting, accomplish the most by doing the least, bears the characteristic stamp of Taoism, the ancient tradition of knowledge that fostered both the healing arts and the martial arts in China. The *Tao-te Ching*, or *The Way and Its Power*, applies the same strategy to society that Sun Tzu attributes to warriors of ancient times:

> Plan for what is difficult while it is easy, do what is great while it is small. The most difficult things in the world must be done while they are still easy, the greatest things in the world must be done while they are still small. For this reason sages never do what is great, and this is why they can achieve that greatness.

Written over two thousand years ago during a period of prolonged civil warfare, *The Art of War* emerged from the same social conditions as some of the greatest classics of Chinese humanism, including the *Tao-te Ching*. Taking a rational rather than an emotional approach to the problem of conflict, Sun Tzu showed how understanding conflict can lead not only to its revolution, but even to its avoidance altogether.

The prominence of Taoist thought in *The Art of War* has been noted by scholars for centuries, and the classic of strategy is recognized in both

*Note again the similarity of Sun Tzu's advice to medical wisdom: to foil the enemies' plots is like keeping healthy so as to be resistant to disease; to ruin their alliances is like avoiding contagion; to attack their armed forces is like taking medicine; to besiege their cities is like performing surgery.

philosophical and political works of the Taoist canon. The level of knowledge represented by the upper reaches of *The Art of War*, the level of invincibility and the level of no conflict, is one expression of what Taoist lore calls "deep knowledge and strong action."

The Book of Balance and Harmony (Chung-ho chi / Zhongho ji), a medieval Taoist work, says, "Deep knowledge of principle knows without seeing, strong practice of the Way accomplishes without striving. Deep knowledge is to 'know without going out the door, see the way of heaven without looking out the window.' Strong action is to 'grow ever stronger, adapting to all situations.'"

In terms of *The Art of War*, the master warrior is likewise the one who knows the psychology and mechanics of conflict so intimately that every move of an opponent is seen through at once, and one who is able to act in precise accord with situations, riding on their natural patterns with a minimum of effort. *The Book of Balance and Harmony* goes on to describe Taoist knowledge and practice further in terms familiar to the quest of the warrior:

> Deep knowledge is to be aware of disturbance before disturbance, to be aware of danger before danger, to be aware of destruction before destruction, to be aware of calamity before calamity. Strong action is training the body without being burdened by the body, exercising the mind without being used by the mind, working in the world without being affected by the world, carrying out tasks without being obstructed by tasks.
>
> By deep knowledge of principle, one can change disturbance into order, change danger into safety, change destruction into survival, change calamity into fortune. By strong action on the Way, one can bring the body to the realm of longevity, bring the mind to the sphere of mystery, bring the world to great peace, and bring tasks to great fulfillment.

As these passages suggest, warriors of Asia who used Taoist or Zen arts to achieve profound calmness did not do so just to prepare their minds to sustain the awareness of imminent death, but also to achieve the sensitivity needed to respond to situations without stopping to ponder. *The Book of Balance and Harmony* says:

ARMORED GUARDIAN
Tang dynasty, 618-907 C.E.

Comprehension in a state of quiescence, accomplishment without striving, knowing without seeing—this is the sense and response of the Transformative Tao. Comprehension in a state of quiescence can comprehend anything, accomplishment without striving can accomplish anything, knowing without seeing can know anything.

As in *The Art of War*, the range of awareness and efficiency of the Taoist adept is unnoticeable, imperceptible to others, because their critical moments take place before ordinary intelligence has mapped out a description of the situation. *The Book of Balance and Harmony* says:

> To sense and comprehend after action is not worthy of being called comprehension. To accomplish after striving is not worthy of being called accomplishment. To know after seeing is not worthy of being called knowing. These three are far from the way of sensing and response.
>
> Indeed, to be able to do something before it exists, sense something before it becomes active, see something before it sprouts, are three abilities that develop interdependently. Then nothing is sensed but is comprehended, nothing is undertaken without response, nowhere does one go without benefit.

One of the purposes of Taoist literature is to help to develop this special sensitivity and responsiveness to master living situations. *The Book of Balance and Harmony* mentions the "Transformative Tao" in reference to the analytical and meditative teachings of the *I Ching*, the locus classicus of the formula for sensitivity and responsiveness. Like the *I Ching* and other classical Taoist literature, *The Art of War* has an incalculable abstract reserve and metaphorical potential. And like other classical Taoist literature, it yields its subtleties in accord with the mentality of the reader and the manner in which it is put into practice.

The association of martial arts with Taoist tradition extends back to the legendary Yellow Emperor of the third millennium B.C.E., one of the major culture heroes of China and an important figure in Taoist lore. According to myth, the Yellow Emperor conquered savage tribes through the use of magical martial arts taught him by a Taoist immortal, and he is also said to have composed the famous *Yin Convergence Clas-*

sic (Yinfu ching / Yinfu jing), a Taoist work of great antiquity traditionally given both martial and spiritual interpretations.

Over a thousand years later, warrior chieftains overthrowing the remnants of ancient Chinese slave society and introducing humanistic concepts of government composed the classic sayings of the *I Ching*, another Taoist text traditionally used as a basis for both martial and civil arts. The basic principles of the *I Ching* figure prominently in Sun Tzu's science of political warfare, just as they are essential to individual combat and defense techniques in the traditional martial arts that grew out of Taoist exercises.

The next great Taoist text after the *Yin Convergence Classic* and *I Ching* was the *Tao-te Ching*, like *The Art of War* a product of the era of the Warring States, which ravaged China in the middle of the first millennium B.C.E. This great classic represents the prevailing attitude toward war that characterizes Sun Tzu's manual: that it is destructive even for the victors, often counterproductive, a reasonable course of action only when there is no choice:

> Those who assist a leader by means of the Tao do not use arms to coerce the world, for these things tend to reverse—brambles grow where an army has been, bad years follow a great war.
>
> Weapons are inauspicious instruments, not the tools of the enlightened. When there is no choice but to use them, it is best to be calm and free from greed, and not celebrate victory. Those who celebrate victory are bloodthirsty, and the bloodthirsty cannot have their way with the world.

In a similar way, *The Art of War* pinpoints anger and greed as fundamental causes of defeat. According to Sun Tzu, it is the unemotional, reserved, calm, detached warrior who wins, not the hothead seeking vengeance and not the ambitious seeker of fortune. *The Tao-te Ching* says:

> Those who are good at knighthood are not militaristic, those who are good at battle do not become angry, those who are good at prevailing over opponents do not get involved.

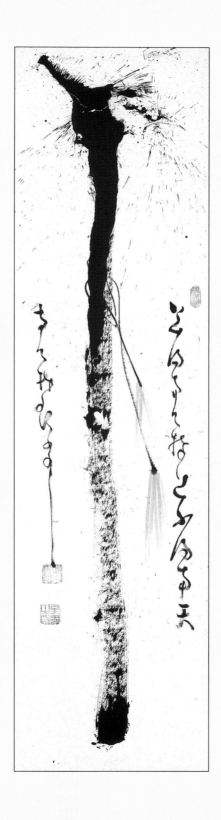

ZEN STAFF
by Nantembo, 1839-1925

The strategy of operating outside the sphere of emotional influence is part of the general strategy of unfathomability that *The Art of War* emphasizes in characteristic Taoist style: Sun Tzu says, "Those skilled in defense hide in the deepest depths of the earth, those skilled in attack maneuver in the highest heights of the sky. Therefore they can preserve themselves and achieve complete victory."

This emphasis on the advantage of enigma pervades Taoist thinking, from the political realm to the realms of commerce and craft, where, it is said, "A good merchant hides his treasures and appears to have nothing," and "A good craftsman leaves no traces." These sayings were adopted by Zen Buddhists to represent their art, and the uncanny approach to the warrior's way was taken up both literally and figuratively by Zen Buddhists, who were among the foremost students of the Taoist classics and developers of esoteric martial arts.

Writings on both the civil and military aspects of political organization are found throughout the Taoist canon. *The Book of the Huainan Masters (Huainanzi / Huai-nan-tzu)*, one of the great Taoist classics of the early Han dynasty, which followed the dramatic end of the Warring States period, includes an entire chapter on Taoist military science that takes up the central theme of the practice of *The Art of War*:

> In martial arts, it is important that strategy be unfathomable, that form be concealed, and that movements be unexpected, so that preparedness against them be impossible.
>
> What enables a good general to win without fail is always having unfathomable wisdom and a modus operandi that leaves no tracks.
>
> Only the formless cannot be affected. Sages hide in unfathomability, so their feelings cannot be observed; they operate in formlessness, so their lines cannot be crossed.

In *The Art of War*, Sun Tzu writes, "Be extremely subtle, even to the point of formlessness. Be extremely mysterious, even to the point of soundlessness. Thereby you can be the director of the opponent's fate."

Both Sun Tzu and the masters of Huainan, a group of Taoist and Confucian sages gathered by a local king, recognize a level of wisdom where conflict does not emerge and victory is not visible to the ordinary eye, but both books are, after all, written in recognition of the difficulty and rarity of this refined attainment. Like Sun Tzu's art of war, the strategy of the masters of Huainan provides for actual conflict, not only as a last resort, but also as an operation to be carried out under the strictest conditions, with appropriate leadership:

> A general must see alone and know alone, meaning that he must see what others do not see and know what others do not know. Seeing what others do not see is called brilliance, knowing what others do not know is called genius. Brilliant geniuses win first, meaning that they defend in such a way as to be unassailable and attack in such a way as to be irresistible.

The rigorous conditions of Taoistic military action are paralleled by those of Taoist spiritual practice. Metaphors of peace and war are widely used in manuals of Taoist meditation and exercise. One of the most basic principles of Taoist practice, deriving from the teachings of the *I Ching*, is the mastery of "emptiness and fullness," which has both physical and psychological implications.

Given an entire chapter in *The Art of War*, the mastery of emptiness and fullness is fundamental to the physical accomplishment of Taoist fighting arts like Absolute Boxing, and to the organizational, or sociopolitical, aspect of the arts of both civil and military government. Explaining the understanding of emptiness and fullness as the Way to certain victory, the masters of Huainan say:

> This is a matter of emptiness and fullness. When there are rifts between superiors and subordinates, when generals and officers are disaffected with each other, and dissatisfaction has built up in the minds of the troops, this is called emptiness. When the civilian leadership is intelligent and the military leadership is good, when superiors and subordinates are of like mind, and will and energy operate together, this is called fullness.
>
> The skilled can fill their people with energy to confront the emptiness of others, while the incompetent drain their people of energy in face of the fullness of others.
>
> When welfare and justice embrace the whole people, when pub-

lic works are sufficient to meet national emergencies, when the policy of selection for office is satisfactory to the intelligent, when planning is sufficient to know strengths and weaknesses, that is the basis of certain victory.

The political basis of military strength, or the social basis of the strength of any organization, is a teaching that is also rooted in the *I Ching*. In *The Art of War* this is given premier importance, as the first item in the first chapter, on strategy, involves examining the Way of an adversary group—the moral fiber, the coherence of the social order, the popularity of the government, or the common morale. Under the right conditions, according to Sun Tzu, a small group could prevail over a large group; and among the conditions that could make this possible were justice, order, cohesion, and morale. This is another pivot of Chinese thought that is also highlighted by the masters of Huainan in the context of military strategy:

> Strength is not just a matter of extensive territory and a large population, victory is not just a matter of efficient armaments, security is not just a matter of high walls and deep moats, authority is not just a matter of strict orders and frequent punishments. Those who establish a viable organization will survive even if they are small, while those who establish a moribund organization will perish even if they are large.

This theme is also emphasized by another of the great military strategists of old China, Zhuge Liang of the third century C.E., who followed the teachings of Sun Tzu to become legendary for his genius:

> The Tao of military operations lies in harmonizing people. When people are in harmony, they will fight naturally, without being exhorted to do so. If the officers and soldiers are suspicious of each other, warriors will not join up; if loyal advice is not heard, small minds will talk and criticize in secret. When hypocrisy sprouts, even if you have the wisdom of ancient warrior kings you could not defeat a peasant, let alone a crowd of them. This is why tradition says, "A military operation is like a fire; if it is not stopped, it will burn itself out."

Zhuge's status as a practical genius is so great that his writings, his designs, and writings about him are actually included in the Taoist canon. Like *The Art of War* and the Taoist classics, Zhuge's philosophy of warfare approaches the positive by way of the negative, in the Taoist fashion of "nondoing":

> In ancient times, those who governed well did not arm, those who were armed well did not set up battle lines, those who set up battle lines well did not fight, those who fought well did not lose, those who lost well did not perish.

This echoes the idea of combat as a last resort, the ideal of winning without fighting offered by *The Art of War*, following the teaching of the *Tao-te Ching*. Zhuge Liang also quotes the classic admonition from this revered Taoist text, "Weapons are instruments of ill omen, to be used only when unavoidable," but he too shares the Taoist historical consciousness that the age of original humanity was already gone, and like Sun Tzu he was personally involved in a time of raging civil war. Zhuge's work in the Taoist canon therefore contains both rational views and practical teachings for political and military security that follow closely on those of ancient Sun Tzu:

> The administration of military affairs means the administration of border affairs, or the administration of affairs in outlying regions, in such a way as to relieve people from major disturbances.
>
> This administration is done by authority and military prowess, executing the violent and rebellious in order to preserve the country and keep the homeland secure. This is why civilization requires the existence of military preparedness.
>
> It is for this reason that beasts have claws and fangs. When they are joyful, they play with each other, when angry they attack each other. Humans have no claws or fangs, so they make armor and weapons to help defend themselves.
>
> So nations have armies to help them, rulers have ministers to assist them. When the helper is strong, the nation is secure; when the helper is weak, the nation is in peril.

Here Zhuge follows Sun Tzu directly, as he does in his emphasis on

HUNTING HORSEMAN
Second or first century B.C.E.

leadership and its popular basis. In Sun Tzu's scheme, both civil and military leadership are among the first conditions to be scrutinized. Zhuge follows Sun Tzu and the masters of Huainan in seeing the strength of leadership based at once on personal qualities and on popular support. In Taoist thought, power was moral as well as material, and it was believed that moral power manifested itself both as self-mastery and as influence over others. To explain the strength of a national defense force, Zhuge writes:

> This in turn depends on the generals entrusted with military leadership. A general that is not popular is not a help to the nation, not a leader of the army.

A general who is "not popular" is one who, according to another way of reading the characters, "denies the people." Sun Tzu emphasizes the unity of wills as a fundamental source of strength, and his minimalist philosophy of warfare is a natural outgrowth of the central idea of common interest; on the basis of this principle, Zhuge Liang again quotes the *Tao-te Ching* to express the ideal of the sage warrior concerned for the body of society as a whole—"Weapons are instruments of ill omen, to be used only when it is unavoidable."

Zhuge also follows *The Art of War* closely in his emphasis on avoiding action without strategy as well as action without need:

> The way to use weapons is to carry out operations only after having first determined your strategy. Carefully examine the patterns of the climate and terrain, and look into the hearts of the people. Train in the use of military equipment, make patterns of rewards and punishments clear, observe the strategy of opponents, watch out for dangerous passes en route, distinguish places of safety and danger, find out the conditions of both sides, be aware of when to advance and when to withdraw, adapt to the timing of circumstances, set up defensive measures while strengthening your attack force, promote soldiers for their ability, draw up plans for success, consider the matter of life and death—only when you have done all this can you send forth armies entrusted to generals that will reach out with the power to capture opponents.

Speed and coordination, central to success in battle according to Sun Tzu's art of war, also derive not only from strategic preparedness, but from the psychological cohesion on which leadership depends; Zhuge writes:

> A general is a commander, a useful tool for a nation. First determining strategy then carrying it out, his command is as though borne afloat on a torrent, his conquest is like a hawk striking its prey. Like a drawn bow when still, like a machine starting up in action, he breaks through wherever he turns, and even powerful enemies perish. If the general has no foresight and the soldiers lack impetus, mere strategy without unification of wills cannot suffice to strike fear into an enemy even if you have a million troops.

Mentioning Sun Tzu's classic as the ultimate manual for successful strategy, Zhuge concludes his essay on military organization by summing up the main points of *The Art of War* as he incorporated them into his own practice, centering on those aspects of the training and mood of warriors that derive from Taoist tradition:

> Have no hard feelings toward anyone who has not shown you enmity, do not fight with anyone who does not oppose you. The effective skill of an engineer can only be seen by the eyes of an expert, the operation of plans in battle can only be set in action through the strategy of Sun Tzu.

Following Sun Tzu, Zhuge emphasizes the advantages of unexpectedness and speed, capable of reversing otherwise insurmountable odds:

> Planning should be secret, attack should be swift. When an army takes its objective like a hawk striking its prey, and battles like a river broken through a dam, its opponents will scatter before the army tires. This is the use of the momentum of an army.

As mentioned before, among the main points of emphasis in Sun

Tzu's art of war is objectivity, and his classic teaches how to assess situations in a dispassionate manner. Zhuge also follows Sun in this, stressing the advantage of carefully calculated action:

> Those who are skilled in combat do not become angered, those who are skilled at winning do not become afraid. Thus the wise win before they fight, while the ignorant fight to win.

Here Zhuge quotes *The Art of War* directly, adding Sun Tzu's warnings about the consequences of poor planning, wasteful actions, and wasteful personnel:

> A country is exhausted when it must buy its supplies at high prices, and is impoverished when it ships supplies long distances. Attacks should not be repeated, battles should not be multiplied. Use strength according to capacity, aware that it will be spent with excessive use. Get rid of the worthless, and the country can be peaceful; get rid of the incompetent, and the country can be profited.

Finally Zhuge goes on in the tradition of the *Tao-te Ching*, *The Art of War*, and *The Masters of Huainan* to give victory to the unfathomable:

> A skilled attack is one against which opponents do not know how to defend; a skilled defense is one which opponents do not know how to attack. Therefore those skilled in defense are not so because of fortress walls.
> This is why high walls and deep moats do not guarantee security, while strong armor and effective weapons do not guarantee strength. If opponents want to hold firm, attack where they are unprepared; if opponents want to establish a battlefront, appear where they do not expect you.

This idea of knowing while being unknown, repeated again and again as a key to success, is one of the strongest links between Taoist meditation and *The Art of War*, for the secret to this art of "invisibility" is precisely the interior detachment cultivated by Taoists for attaining impersonal views of objective reality. Certain of the philosophical teachings of early Taoism are commonly used in practical schools as codes for exercises used in personal cultivation.

Understanding the practical aspect of Taoist philosophical teachings helps to cut through the sense of paradox that may be caused by seemingly contradictory attitudes. That Sun Tzu calmly teaches the ruthless art of war while condemning war may seem contradictory if this fact is seen outside the context of the total understanding of the human mentality fostered by Taoist learning.

The simultaneous appreciation of very different points of view is a powerful Taoist technique, whose understanding can resolve contradiction and paradox. The model of the paradox of *The Art of War* can be seen in the *Tao-te Ching*, where both ruthlessness and kindness are part of the Way of the sage.

"Heaven and earth are not humanistic—they regard myriad beings as straw dogs; sages are not humanistic—they regard people as straw dogs," wrote the philosopher of the *Tao-te Ching*. A horrified Western Sinologist working in the 1950s, shortly after the truce in Korea, wrote that this passage had "unleashed a monster," but to a Taoist this statement does not represent inhumanity but an exercise in objectivity, similar to Buddhist exercises in impersonality.

In modern terms, this sort of statement is no different from that of a psychologist or sociologist making the observation that the attitudes, thoughts, and expectations of entire nations are not arrived at purely by a multitude of independent rational decisions, but largely under the influence of environmental factors beyond the control of the individual or even the community.

As Sun Tzu's classic attests, the place of such an observation in the art of war is not to cultivate a callous or bloodthirsty attitude, but to understand the power of mass psychology. Understanding how people can be manipulated through emotions, for example, is as useful for those who wish to avoid this as it is for those who wish to practice it.

Seen in this light, *The Art of War* is no more a call to arms than a study on conditioning is a recommendation for slavery. By so thoroughly analyzing the political, psychological, and material factors involved in

DEMON GENERALS OF THE TAOIST WATER DEITY. Ming dynasty, 1368–1644

conflict, Sun Tzu's professed aim was not to encourage warfare but to minimize and curtail it.

An impersonal view of humanity as not the master of its own fate may be necessary to liberate a warrior from emotional entanglements that might precipitate irrational approaches to conflict; but it is not, in the Taoist scheme of things, held to justify destructive behavior. The counterbalance to this view is also found in the *Tao-te Ching* prefiguring Sun Tzu's teachings in *The Art of War*:

> I have three treasures that I keep and prize: one is kindness, second is frugality, and third is not presuming to take precedence over others. By kindness one can be brave, by frugality one can reach out, and by not presuming to take precedence one can survive effectively. If one gives up kindness and courage, gives up frugality and breadth, and gives up humility for aggressiveness, one will die. The exercise of kindness in battle leads to victory, the exercise of kindness in defense leads to security.

In his classic Master Sun likens military action to a "fire, which burns itself out if not stopped," and if his strategy of success without conflict was not always attainable, his strategy of hyperefficiency could at least minimize senseless violence and destruction. In Taoist terms, success is often gained by not doing, and the strategy of *The Art of War* is as much in knowing what not to do and when not to do it as it is in knowing what to do and when to do it.

The art of not doing—which includes the unobtrusiveness, unknowability, and ungraspability at the core of esoteric Asian martial arts—belongs to the branch of Taoism known as the science of essence. The arts of doing—which include the external techniques of both cultural and martial arts—belong to the branch of Taoism known as the science of life. The science of essence has to do with state of mind, the science of life has to do with use of energy. Like a classic Taoist text, it is in true balance of these two that *The Art of War* is most completely understood.

In more modern times, the definitive Taoist statement on this subject is immortalized in *Journey to the West (Hsi-yu chi / Xiyou ji)*, one of the Four Extraordinary Books of the Ming dynasty (1368–1644). Drawing on earlier Taoist sources from wartime China under the duress of Mongol invasions, this remarkable novel is a classic representation of the result of what in Taoist terms would be called studying the science of life without the science of essence, material development without corresponding psychological development, or in Sun Tzu's terms having force without intelligence.

The central figure of this novel is a magical monkey who founds a monkey civilization and becomes its leader by establishing a territory for the monkeys. Subsequently the monkey king overcomes a "devil confusing the world," and steals the devil's sword.

Returning to his own land with the devil's sword, the monkey king takes up the practice of swordsmanship. He even teaches his monkey subjects to make toy weapons and regalia to play at war.

Unfortunately, though ruler of a nation, the martial monkey king is not yet ruler of himself. In eminently logical backward reasoning, the monkey reflects that if neighboring nations note the monkeys' play, they might assume the monkeys were preparing for war. In that case, they might therefore take preemptive action against the monkeys, who would then be faced with real warfare armed only with toy weapons.

Thus, the monkey king thoughtfully initiates the arms race, ordering pre-preemptive stockpiling of real weapons.

If it seems disconcerting to read a thirteenth-century description of twentieth-century politics, it may be no less so to read a book as old as the Bible describing tactics in use today not only by guerrilla warriors but by influential politicians and corporate executives. Following the disillusionist posture of the *Tao-te Ching* and *The Art of War*, the story of the monkey king also prefigures a major movement in modern scientific thought following the climax of the Western divorce of religion and science centuries ago.

The monkey king in the story exercised power without wisdom, disrupting the natural order and generally raising hell until he ran into the limits of matter, where he was finally trapped. There he lost the excitement of impulsive enthusiasm, and he was eventually released to seek the science of essence, under the strict condition that his knowledge and power were to be controlled by compassion, the expression of wisdom and unity of being.

The monkey's downfall finally comes about when he meets Buddha, whom the Taoist celestial immortals summon to deal with the intractable beast. The immortals had attempted to "cook" him in the "cauldron of the eight trigrams," that is, to put him through the training of spiritual alchemy based on the Taoist *I Ching*, but he had jumped out still unrefined.

Buddha conquers the monkey's pride by demonstrating the insuperable law of universal relativity and has him imprisoned in "the mountain of the five elements," the world of matter and energy, where he suffers the results of his arrogant antics.

After five hundred years, at length Guanyin (Kuan Yin), the transhistorical Buddhist saint traditionally honored as the personification of universal compassion, shows up at the prison of the now repentant monkey and recites this telling verse:

Too bad the magic monkey didn't serve the public
As he madly flaunted heroics in days of yore.
With a cheating heart he made havoc
In the gathering of immortals;
With grandiose gall he went for his ego
To the heaven of happiness.
Among a hundred thousand troops,
None could oppose him;
In the highest heavens above
He had a threatening presence.
But since he was stymied on meeting our Buddha,
When will he ever reach out and show his achievements again?

Now the monkey pleads with the saint for his release. The saint grants this on the condition that the monkey devote himself to the quest for higher enlightenment, not only for himself but for society at large. Finally, before letting the monkey go to set out on the long road ahead, as a precaution the saint places a ring around the monkey's head, a ring that will tighten and cause the monkey severe pain whenever a certain spell invoking compassion is said in response to any new misbehavior on the part of the monkey.

The Art of War has been known for a hundred generations as the

THE KINGDOM OF THE FISHES
Eastern Han dynasty, 25–220 C.E.

foremost classic of strategy; but perhaps its greatest wizardry lies in the ring of compassion that Master Sun slips over the head of every warrior who tries to use this book. And as history shows, the magic spell that tightens its grip is chanted whenever a warrior forgets the ring.

THE STRUCTURE AND CONTENT OF THE ART OF WAR

The Art of War, permeated with the philosophical and political thought of the *Tao-te Ching*, also resembles the great Taoist classic in that it is largely composed of a collection of aphorisms commonly attributed to a shadowy, semilegendary author. Certain Taoists regard the *Tao-te Ching*, to be a transmissions of ancient lore compiled and elaborated by its "author," rather than a completely original work, and the same may very well be true of *The Art of War*. In any case, both classics share the general pattern of central themes recurring throughout the text in different contexts.

The first book of *The Art of War* is devoted to the importance of strategy. As the classic *I Ching* says, "Leaders plan in the beginning when they do things," and "Leaders consider problems and prevent them." In terms of military operations, *The Art of War* brings up five things that are to be assessed before undertaking any action: the Way, the weather, the terrain, the military leadership, and discipline.

In this context, the Way (Tao) has to do with civil leadership, or rather the relationship between political leadership and the populace. In both Taoist and Confucian parlance, a righteous government is described as "imbued with the Tao," and Sun Tzu the martialist similarly speaks of the Way as "inducing the people to have the same aim as the leadership."

Assessment of the weather, the question of the season for action, also relates to concern for the people, meaning both the populace in general as well as military personnel. The essential point here is to avoid disruption of the productive activities of the people, which depend on the seasons, and to avoid extremes of weather that would handicap or harm troops in the field.

The terrain is to be sized up in terms of distance, degree of difficulty of travel, dimensions, and safety. The use of scouts and native guides is important here, for, as the *I Ching* says, "Chasing game without a guide leads one into the bush."

The criteria offered by *The Art of War* for assessment of the military leadership are traditional virtues also much emphasized in Confucianism and medieval Taoism: intelligence, trustworthiness, humaneness, courage, and sternness. According to the great Chan Buddhist Fushan, "Humaneness without intelligence is like having a field but not plowing it. Intelligence without courage is like having sprouts but not weeding. Courage without humaneness is like knowing how to reap but not how to sow." The other two virtues, trustworthiness and sternness, are those by which the leadership wins both the loyalty and obedience of the troops.

The fifth item to be assessed, discipline, refers to organizational coherence and efficiency. Discipline is very much connected with the virtues of trustworthiness and sternness sought after in military leaders, since it uses the corresponding mechanisms of reward and punishment. A great deal of emphasis is placed on the establishment of a clear system of rewards and punishments accepted by the warriors as fair and impartial. This was one of the main points of Legalism, a school of thought that also arose during the Warring States period, stressing the importance of rational organization and the rule of law rather than personalistic feudal government.

Following a discussion of these five assessments, *The Art of War* goes on to emphasize the central importance of deception: "A military operation involves deception. Even though you are competent, appear incompetent. Though effective, appear ineffective." As the *Tao-te Ching* says, "One with great skill appears inept." The element of surprise, so important for victory with maximum efficiency, depends on knowing others while being unknown to others, so secrecy and misdirection are considered essential arts.

Generally speaking, the toe-to-toe battle is the last resort of the skilled warrior, who Sun Tzu says should be prepared but should nevertheless avoid confrontation with a strong opponent. Rather than trying to overwhelm opponents directly, Master Sun recommends wearing them down by flight, fostering disharmony within their ranks, manipulating their feelings, and using their anger and pride against them. Thus, in sum, the opening statement of *The Art of War* introduces the three main facets of the warrior's art: the social, the psychological, and the physical.

The second chapter of *The Art of War*, on doing battle, stresses the domestic consequences of war, even foreign war. Emphasis is on speed and efficiency, with strong warnings not to prolong operations, especially far afield. Considerable attention is devoted to the importance of conservation of energy and material resources. In order to minimize the drain of war on the economy and population, Sun Tzu recommends the practice of feeding off the enemy and using captive forces won over by good treatment.

The third chapter, on planning a siege, also emphasizes conservation—the general aim is to gain victory while keeping as much intact as possible, both socially and materially, rather than destroying whoever and whatever stands in the way. In this sense Master Sun affirms that it is best to win without fighting.

Several tactical recommendations follow in pursuit of this general conservative principle. First of all, since it is desirable to win without battle, Sun Tzu says that it is best to overcome opponents at the outset by foiling their plans. Failing that, he recommends isolating opponents and rendering them helpless. Here again it would seem that time is of the essence, but the point is made that speed does not mean haste, and thorough preparation is necessary. And when victory is won, Sun stresses that it should be complete, to avoid the expense of maintaining an occupation force.

The chapter goes on to outline strategies for action according to relative numbers of protagonists versus antagonists, again observing that it is wise to avoid taking on unfavorable odds if possible. The *I Ching* says, "It is unlucky to be stubborn in the face of insurmountable odds." Furthermore, while the formulation of strategy depends on prior intelligence, it is also imperative to adapt to actual battle situations; as the *I Ching* says, "Coming to an impasse, change; having changed, you can get through."

Master Sun then makes note of five ways to ascertain victory, pur-

THE CONQUESTS OF THE EMPEROR QIANLONG

Ch'ing dynasty, 1644–1911

Copyright © 1995 by Sotheby's Inc., New York

suant to the theme that skillful warriors fight only when assured of winning. According to Sun, the victors are those who know when to fight
and when not to fight; those who know when to use many or few
troops; those whose officers and soldiers are of one mind; those who
face the unprepared with preparation; and those with able generals who
are not constrained by government.

This last point is a very delicate one, as it places an even greater
moral and intellectual responsibility on the military leadership. While
war is never to be initiated by the military itself, as later explained, but
by the command of the civilian government, Sun Tzu says an absentee
civilian leadership that interferes ignorantly with field command "takes
away victory by deranging the military."

Again the real issue seems to be that of knowledge; the premise
that military leadership in the field should not be subject to interfer-
ence by civilian government is based on the idea that the key to victory is intimate knowledge of the actual situation. Outlining these five
ways to determine which side is likely to prevail, Sun Tzu states that
when you know both yourself and others you are never in danger,
when you know yourself but not others you have half a chance of winning, and when you know neither yourself nor others you are in danger in every battle.

The fourth chapter of *The Art of War* is on formation, one of the
most important issues of strategy and combat. In a characteristically
Taoist posture, Sun Tzu here asserts that the keys to victory are adaptability and inscrutability. As the commentator Du Mu explains, "The inner condition of the formless is inscrutable, whereas that of those who
have adopted a specific form is obvious. The inscrutable win, the obvious lose."

Inscrutability in this context is not purely passive, does not simply
mean being withdrawn or concealed from others; more important, it
means perception of what is invisible to others and response to possibil-
ities not yet discerned by those who look only at the obvious. By seeing opportunities before they are visible to others and being quick to
act, the uncanny warrior can take situations by the throat before matters get out of hand.

Following this line of thought, Sun Tzu reemphasizes the pursuit of certain victory by knowing when to act and when not to act. Make yourself invincible, he says, and take on opponents only when they are vulnerable: "Good warriors take their stand on ground where they cannot lose, and do not overlook conditions that make an opponent prone to defeat." Reviewing these conditions, Sun rephrases some of his guidelines for assessment of organizations, such as discipline and ethics versus rapacity and corruption.

The topic of the fifth chapter of *The Art of War* is force, or momentum, the dynamic structure of a group in action. Here Master Sun emphasizes organizational skills, coordination, and the use of both orthodox and guerrilla methods of war. He stresses change and surprise, employing endless variations of tactics, using opponents' psychological conditions to maneuver them into vulnerable positions.

The essence of Sun Tzu's teaching on force is unity and coherence in an organization, using the force of momentum rather than relying on individual qualities and talents: "Good warriors seek effectiveness in battle from the force of momentum, not from individual people."

It is this recognition of the power of the group to even out internal disparities and function as one body of force that sets *The Art of War* apart from the idiosyncratic individualism of the samurai swordsmen of late feudal Japan, whose stylized martial arts are so familiar in the West. This emphasis is one of the essential features that has made Sun Tzu's ancient work so useful for the corporate warriors of modern Asia, among whom *The Art of War* is widely read and still regarded as the matchless classic of strategy in conflict.

The sixth chapter takes up the subject of "emptiness and fullness," already noted as fundamental Taoist concepts commonly adapted to martial arts. The idea is to be filled with energy while at the same time draining opponents, in order, as Master Sun says, to make oneself invincible and take on opponents only when they are vulnerable. One of the simplest of these tactics is well known not only in the context of war, but also in social and business maneuvering: "Good warriors get others to come to them, and do not go to others."

Conserving one's own energy while inducing others to dissipate theirs is another function of the inscrutability so highly prized by the Taoist warrior: "The consummation of forming an army is to arrive at formlessness," says Master Sun, for then no one can formulate a strategy against you. At the same time, he says, induce opponents to construct their own formations, get them to spread themselves thin; test opponents to gauge their resources and reactions, but remain unknown yourself.

In this case, formlessness and fluidity are not merely means of defense and surprise, but means of preserving dynamic potential, energy that could easily be lost by trying to hold on to a specific position or formation. Master Sun likens a successful force to water, which has no constant form but, as the *Tao-te Ching* notes, prevails over everything in spite of its apparent weakness: Sun says, "A military force has no constant formation, water has no constant shape. The ability to gain victory by changing and adapting according to the opponent is called genius."

The seventh chapter of *The Art of War*, on armed struggle, dealing with concrete field organization and combat maneuvers, recapitulates several of Sun Tzu's main themes. Beginning with the need for information and preparation, Sun says, "Act after having made assessments. The one who first knows the measures of far and near wins—this is the rule of armed struggle." The *I Ching* says, "Be prepared, and you will be lucky."

Again expounding his characteristic minimalist/essentialist tactical philosophy, Sun Tzu goes on to say, "Take away the energy of opposing armies, take away the heart of their generals." Echoing his teachings on emptiness and fullness, he also says, "Avoid keen energy, strike the slumping and receding." To take full advantage of the principles of emptiness and fullness, Sun teaches four kinds of mastery essential to the uncanny warrior: mastery of energy, mastery of the heart, mastery of strength, and mastery of adaptation.

The principles of emptiness and fullness also display the fundamental mechanism of the classic yin-yang principles on which they are based, that of reversion from one to the other at the extremes. Master Sun says, "Do not stop an army on its way home. A surrounded army must be given a way out. Do not press a desperate enemy." The I Ching says, "The sovereign uses three chasers, letting the game ahead escape," and "if you are too adamant, action is unlucky, even if you are right."

The eighth chapter of *The Art of War* is devoted to adaptation, already seen to be one of the cornerstones of the warrior's art. Master Sun says, "If generals do not know how to adapt advantageously, even if they know the lay of the land they cannot take advantage of it." The *I Ching* says, "Persist too intensely at what is currently beyond your depth, and your fidelity to that course will bring misfortune, no gain."

Adaptability naturally depends on readiness, another persistent theme of *The Art of War*. Master Sun says, "The rule of military operations is not to count on opponents not coming, but to rely on having ways of dealing with them; not to count on opponents not attacking, but to rely on having what cannot be attacked." The *I Ching* says, "If you take on too much without a solid foundation, you will eventually be drained, leaving you with embarrassment and bad luck."

In *The Art of War*, readiness does not just mean material preparedness; without a suitable mental state, sheer physical power is not enough to guarantee victory. Master Sun here defines the psychological dimensions of the victorious leader indirectly, by enumerating five dangers—to be too willing to die, too eager to live, too quick to anger, too puritanical, or too sentimental. Any one of these excesses, he affirms, create vulnerabilities that can easily be exploited by canny opponents. The *I Ching* says, "When waiting on the fringes of a situation, before the appropriate time to go into action has arrived, be steady and avoid giving in to impulse—then you won't go wrong."

The ninth chapter deals with maneuvering armies. Again Master Sun deals with all three aspects of the warrior's art—the physical, social, and psychological. In concrete physical terms, he begins by recommending certain obvious types of terrain that enhance the odds of victory: high ground, upstream, the sunny side of hills, regions with plenty of resources. Referring to all three dimensions, he then describes ways of interpreting enemy movements.

Although Master Sun never dismisses the weight of sheer numbers or material might, here as elsewhere there is the strong suggestion that social and psychological factors can overcome the sort of power that can be physically quantified: "In military matters it is not necessarily beneficial to have more, only to avoid acting aggressively; it is enough to consolidate your power, assess opponents, and win people, that is all." The *I Ching* says, "When you have means but are not getting anywhere, seek

HANIWA
WARRIOR
Late Tomb
period,
450–710 C.E.

appropriate associates, and you will be lucky." Similarly emphasizing directed group effort, *The Art of War* says, "The individualist without strategy who takes opponents lightly will inevitably become a captive."

Solidarity calls especially for mutual understanding and rapport between the leadership and the followers, achieved through both education and training. The Confucian sage Mencius said, "Those who send people on military operations without educating them ruin them." Master Sun says, "Direct them through cultural arts, unify them through martial arts; this means certain victory." The *I Ching* says, "It is lucky when the rulers nourish the ruled, watching them and bringing out their talents."

The tenth chapter, on terrain, continues the ideas of tactical maneuvering and adaptability, outlining types of terrain and appropriate ways of adjusting to them. It requires some thought to transfer the patterns of these types of terrain to other contexts, but the essential point is in consideration of the relationship of the protagonist to the configurations of the material, social, and psychological environment.

Master Sun follows this with remarks about fatal organizational deficiencies for which the leadership is responsible. Here again emphasis is on the morale of unity: "Look upon your soldiers as beloved children, and they willingly die with you." The *I Ching* says, "Those above secure their homes by kindness to those below." Nevertheless, extending the metaphor, Master Sun also warns against being overly indulgent, with the result of having troops who are like spoiled children.

Intelligence, in the sense of preparatory knowledge, is also stressed in this chapter, where it is particularly defined as including clear awareness of the capabilities of one's forces, the vulnerabilities of opponents, and the lay of the land: "When you know yourself and others, victory is not in danger; when you know sky and earth, victory is inexhaustible." The *I Ching* says, "Be careful in the beginning, and you have no trouble in the end."

The eleventh chapter, entitled "Nine Grounds," presents a more detailed treatment of terrain, particularly in terms of the relationship of a group to the terrain. Again, these "nine grounds" can be understood to apply not only to simple physical territory, but also to "territory" in its social and more abstract senses.

The nine grounds enumerated by Master Sun in this chapter are called a ground of dissolution, light ground, ground of contention, trafficked ground, intersecting ground, heavy ground, bad ground, surrounded ground, and dying (or deadly) ground.

A ground of dissolution is a stage of internecine warfare or civil strife. Light ground refers to shallow incursion into others' territory. A ground of contention is a position that would be advantageous to either side of a conflict. Trafficked ground is where there is free travel. Intersecting ground is territory controlling important arteries of communication. Heavy ground, in contrast to light ground, refers to deep incursion into others' territory. Bad ground is difficult or useless terrain. Surrounded ground has restricted access, suited to ambush. Dying ground is a situation in which it is necessary to fight at once or be annihilated.

Describing the tactics appropriate to each type of ground, Master Sun includes consideration of the social and psychological elements of conflict, insofar as these are inextricably bound up with response to the environment: "Adaptation to different grounds, advantages of contraction and expansion, patterns of human feelings and conditions—these must be examined."

The twelfth chapter of *The Art of War*, on fire attack, begins with a brief description of various kinds of incendiary attack, along with technical considerations and strategies for follow-up.

Perhaps because fire is in an ordinary material sense the most vicious form of martial art (explosives existed but were not used militarily in Sun Tzu's time), it is in this chapter that the most impassioned plea for humanity is found, echoing the Taoist idea that "weapons are instruments of misfortune to be used only when unavoidable." Abruptly ending his short discussion of incendiary attack, Master Sun says, "A government should not mobilize an army out of anger, military leaders should not provoke war out of wrath. Act when it is beneficial to do so, desist if not. Anger can revert to joy, wrath can revert to delight, but a nation destroyed cannot be restored to existence, and the dead cannot be restored to life."

The thirteenth and final chapter of *The Art of War* deals with espionage, thus coming full circle to link up with the opening chapter on strategy, for which intelligence is essential. Again turning to the efficiency-oriented minimalism and conservatism toward which the skills he teaches are directed, Master Sun begins by speaking of the importance of intelligence agents in most emphatic terms: "A major military operation is a severe drain on the nation, and may be kept up for years in the struggle for one day's victory. So to fail to know the conditions of opponents because of reluctance to give rewards for intelligence is extremely inhumane."

Sun goes on to define five kinds of spy, or secret agent. The local spy is one who is hired from among the populace of a region in which operations are planned. An inside spy is one who is hired from among the officials of an opposing regime. A reverse spy is a double agent, hired from among enemy spies. A dead spy is one who is sent in to convey false information. A living spy is one who comes and goes with information.

Here again there is a very strong social and psychological element in Sun Tzu's understanding of the practical complexities of espionage from the point of view of the leadership. Beginning with the issue of leadership, *The Art of War* also ends with the observation that the effective use of spies depends on the leadership. Master Sun says, "One cannot use spies without sagacity and knowledge, one cannot use spies without humanity and justice, one cannot get the truth from spies without subtlety," and he concludes, "Only a brilliant ruler or a wise general who can use the highly intelligent for espionage is sure of great success."

HISTORICAL BACKGROUND

The Art of War was evidently written during the so-called Warring States period of ancient China, which lasted from the fifth to the third century B.C.E. This was a time of protracted disintegration of the Chou (Zhou) dynasty, which had been founded over five hundred years earlier by the political sages who wrote the *I Ching*. The collapse of the ancient order was marked by destabilization of interstate relationships and interminable warfare among aspirants to hegemony in the midst of ever-shifting patterns of alliance and opposition.

A preface to *Strategies of the Warring States (Zhanguo ce / Chan kuo ts'e)*, a classic collection of stories about the political and military affairs of the feudal states of this time, provides a graphic description of the Warring States period:

> Usurpers set themselves up as lords and kings, states run by pretenders and plotters set up armies to make themselves superpowers. Increasingly they imitated one another in this, and their posterity followed their example, Eventually they engulfed and destroyed each other, colluding with larger territories and annexing smaller territories, passing years in violent military operations, filling the fields with bloodshed. Fathers and sons were not close to each other, brothers were not secure with each other, husbands and wives separated—no one could safeguard his or her life. Virtue disappeared. In later years this grew increasingly extreme, with seven large states and five small states contesting each other for power. In general, this was because the Warring States were shamelessly greedy, struggling insatiably to get ahead.

The great humanist philosopher and educator Confucius, who lived right on the eve of the Warring States era, spent his life working against the deterioration in human values that marked the fall of his society into centuries of conflict. In the classic *Analects of Confucius*, the imminent dawn of the Warring States period is presaged in a symbolic vignette of Confucius' encounter with a ruler whom he tried to advise: "Lord Ling of the state of Wei asked Confucius about battle formations. Confucius replied, 'I have learned about the disposition of ritual vessels, but I have not studied military matters,' and left the next day."

This story, as if representing the disappearance of humanity ("Confucius left the next day") from the thoughts and considerations of rulers in the coming centuries of war, is taken up by the Taoist philosopher

LAO-TZU RIDING AN OX, by Zhang Lu, 1464–1538

THE ART OF WAR

Chuang-tzu, who lived in the fourth and third centuries B.C.E., right in the midst of the Warring States period. According to Chuang-tzu's enlargement on the theme, Yen Hui, the most enlightened disciple of Confucius, went to the teacher and asked about going to the state of Wei. Confucius said, "What are you going to do there?"

Yen Hui said, "I have heard that while the ruler of Wei is in the prime of life, his behavior is arbitrary—he exploits his country whimsically and does not see his own mistakes. He exploits his people frivolously, even unto death. Countless masses have died in that state, and the people have nowhere to turn. I have heard you say, 'Leave an orderly state, go to a disturbed state—at the physician's gate, many are the ailing.' I would like to use what I have learned to consider the guidance it offers, so that the state of Wei might be healed."

Confucius said, "You are bent on going, but you will only be punished."

Very few people of the time listened to the pacifistic humanism of Confucius and Mencius. Some say they did not listen because they could not implement the policies advocated by the original Confucians; others say they could not implement the policies because they did not listen, because they did not really want to be humane and just.

Those who listened to the pacifistic humanism of Lao-tzu and Chuang-tzu, on the other hand, generally concealed themselves and worked on the problem from different angles. Lao-tzu and Chuang-tzu show that the man of aggressive violence appears to be ruthless but is really an emotionalist; then they slay the emotionalist with real ruthlessness before revealing the spontaneous nature of free humanity.

The ancient Taoist masters show how real ruthlessness, the coldness of complete objectivity, always includes oneself in its cutting assessment of the real situation. The historical Buddha, a contemporary of Confucius who himself came from a clan of warriors in a time when the warrior caste was consolidating its political dominance, said that conflict would cease if we would be aware of our own death.

This is the ruthlessness of Lao-tzu when he says that the universe is inhumane and the sage sees people as being like the straw dogs used for ritual sacrifices. Chuang-tzu also gives numerous dramatic illustrations of ruthlessness toward oneself as an exercise in perspective designed to lead to cessation of internal and external conflict.

This "inhumanity" is not used by the original philosophers as a justification for quasi-ruthless possessive aggression, but as a meditation on the ultimate meaninglessness of the greed and possessiveness that underlie aggression.

In India, Buddhist aspirants used to visit burning grounds and watch the corpses of those whose families couldn't afford a cremation rot away. This they did to terrify the greed and possessiveness out of themselves. After that they turned their minds toward thoughts of ideal individuals and ideal societies.

Similarly, Master Sun has his readers dwell on the ravages of war, from its incipient phases of treachery and alienation to its extreme forms of incendiary attack and siege, viewed as a sort of mass cannibalism of human and natural resources. With this device he gives the reader an enhanced feeling for the significance of individual and social virtues espoused by the humanitarian pacifists.

From this point of view, it is natural to think of the Taoist thread in *The Art of War* not as a random cultural element, but as key to understanding the text at all of its levels. By the nature of its overt subject matter, *The Art of War* commanded the attention of people who were less likely to pay serious mind to the pacifistic teachings of the classical humanists.

Just as the *I Ching* preserved certain philosophical ideas through all sorts of political and social change through its popularity as an oracle and book of advice, so did *The Art of War* preserve a core of Taoist practical philosophy from destruction by its antithesis.

Paradox is often thought of as a standard device of Taoist psychology, used to cross imperceptible barriers of awareness. Perhaps the paradox of *The Art of War* is in its opposition to war. And as *The Art of War* wars against war, it does so by its own principles; it infiltrates the enemy's lines, uncovers the enemy's secrets, and changes the hearts of the enemy's troops.

THE COMMENTATORS

The commentaries in this translation are selected from a standard collection of eleven interpreters.

CAO CAO (TS'AO TS'AO, 155-200 C.E.)

Cao Cao is one of the most distinguished military figures of Chinese history. Known for his keen intellect and his cunning, Cao received an honorary degree for social virtues and began his official career at the age of twenty. He held a number of important military posts and particularly distinguished himself in a campaign against rebels when he was about thirty years old.

After this he was given a local ministerial position, but was soon recalled to the region of the capital to take up a regional governorship. Citing health reasons, Cao Cao declined the governorship and returned to his homeland. When one of the most violent generals of the Han dynasty deposed the reigning emperor to set up his own puppet, however, Cao Cao came out of retirement, spending his family fortune to raise a private army in opposition to that general.

Subsequently promoted to high office by the emperor, Cao Cao overthrew would-be usurpers and became a general of the highest rank. He was eventually ennobled and was even encouraged to formally take over the throne of the crumbling Han dynasty, but Cao Cao would not do this, likening himself to King Wen of the ancient Chou dynasty, one of the authors of the *I Ching*, a civil and military leader whose personal qualities, social policies, and political accomplishments won a loyal following that formed the basis of the nascent Chou dynasty, but who never set himself up as supreme leader.

Cao Cao was known for his heroism, talent, and strategy, in which he mainly followed the teachings of Sun Tzu's classic, *The Art of War*. In the tradition of the ancient chivalric code, according to which Chinese

THE TEN GREAT GENERALS, dated 1454

ghts were to be learned in both martial and cultural arts, in addition
his military accomplishments Cao Cao was fond of literature and is
d to have made a habit of reading every day, even during military
mpaigns.

NG SHI (LIANG DYNASTY, 502-556)

ng Shi, or "Mr. Meng," is apparently known only for his commen-
y on *The Art of War*. His time was marked by civil war and massive
fering.

LIN (TANG DYNASTY, 618-906)

Lin seems to be known only for his commentary on *The Art of War*.
ring the Tang dynasty, China enlarged its empire, extending its cul-
al and political influence over other peoples, some of whom eventu-
y used their experience under Chinese rule to take over large parts of
ina themselves. Tang-dynasty China also helped establish national
vernments in Japan, Tibet, and Yunnan.

QUAN (TANG DYNASTY, 618-906)

Quan was a devotee of Taoism as well as the martial arts. He lived
the Mountain of Few Abodes, where Bodhidharma, the semilegendary
nder of Chan Buddhism, lived during his last years in China. Taoist
dition attributes Shaolin boxing, a popular school of martial arts, to
s same Bodhidharma. Li Quan was a student of the *Yin Convergence Clas-*
(*Yinfu jing*), a Taoist text attributed to antiquity and traditionally in-
preted in both martial and cultural terms. He is said to have read this
onic text thousands of times without understanding its meaning. Later
went to Black Horse Mountain, the famous site of the tomb of the
st Emperor of China, where he met an old woman who gave him a
rm and explained the meaning of the classic to him. This woman is
ntified with the Old Woman of Black Horse Mountain of folklore,
o was said to have been a ruler of ancient times, considered a Taoist
mortal by the people of the Tang dynasty. Whatever the true identity
his mentor may have been, Li Quan is known for his military strat-
y and wrote a commentary on the *Yin Convergence Classic* from that point
view. Eventually he went into the mountains to study Taoism.

Du You (735-812)

Du You served as an official military advisor, war councillor, and military inspector in several regions. Later in life he also held distinguished posts in the central government, but he eventually gave up office.

Du Mu (803-852)

Du Mu was the grandson of the aforementioned Du You. Known as a "knight of unflinching honesty and extraordinary honor," he earned an advanced academic degree and served in several positions at the imperial court. His fortunes declined in his later years, and he died at the age of fifty. On his deathbed he composed his own epitaph and burned all of his writings. He was known as an outstanding poet.

Zhang Yu (Sung Dynasty, 960-1278)

Zhang Yu is known only for his commentary on *The Art of War* and a collection of biographies of military leaders. The Sung dynasty was a time of more or less constantly increasing pressure from north Asia, culminating in the loss of its ancient homeland and finally all of the continental Chinese empire, to Mongolian invaders.

Mei Yaochen (1002-1060)

Mei Yaochen served in both local and central governments of the new Sung dynasty that followed several generations of disunity after the collapse of the Tang dynasty, and was chosen as one of the compilers and editors of the documents of the Tang dynasty. Mei was a literary correspondent of the famous poet Ou Yangxiu, and was himself a distinguished writer.

Wang Xi (Sung Dynasty, Early Eleventh Century)

Wang Xi was a scholar in the Hanlin or Imperial Academy. He is the author of two books on the *Spring and Autumn Annals* (*Qunqiu / Ch'uh-ch'iu*), one of the Confucian classics of ancient illustrative history. While Sung dynasty China was beset with endless political, economic, and military problems, its culture was very lively, with important new developments in Confucianism, Taoism, and Zen Buddhism. These new forms of practical philosophy exerted a strong influence not only on the Chinese people themselves but even on the non-Chinese peoples who were taking over political control in China, to say nothing of the Koreans, Vietnamese, and Japanese who were watching the continental mainland and were experimenting with these new forms of high culture from China.

CHEN HAO (SUNG DYNASTY, EARLY TWELFTH CENTURY)
Chen Hao was known for his extraordinary personal independence and his great aspirations. He became an officer of the state when he was only twenty years old. When the Jurchen people of north Asia invaded China in the mid 1220s, Chen assembled a patriotic army to defend the homeland. Later he also raised an army in secret to put down an attempted coup by a usurper.

HO YANXI (SUNG DYNASTY)
Nothing seems to be known of Ho Yanxi other than that he lived during the Sung dynasty and wrote this commentary on *The Art of War*.

THE TRANSLATION

The language of the Chinese classics is different from that of even the earliest commentators, very different from that of the Tang and Sung writers, vastly different from modern Chinese. All Chinese classics, extensively studied as they are, contain words and passages interpreted differently among Chinese commentators themselves. These differences in reading and understanding are sometimes radical. It is only natural, therefore, that translations of ancient Chinese texts into modern Western languages, which differ so greatly from Chinese, should themselves exhibit a considerable range of variety.

This is especially true considering the pregnancy of the Chinese language and the abundant use of imagery and allusion in Chinese literature. There are many choices of techniques available to the translator for conveying the contents of classical Chinese writings to the reader in another language. In twenty years of translating, never have I seen or translated an Oriental classic that I did not find so rich as to be able to generate at least three possible translations.

There are, again, various options available for dealing with this situation. As in my other translations from Oriental classics, the technical aim of my approach to *The Art of War* has been to make the flesh transparent and the bones stand out, to reproduce an abstract form to be filled with the colors of the individual reader's own life situations. Therefore I have omitted some references to certain local content, such items as ancient Chinese weaponry, not as being without a certain interest, but as incidental to the question of present-day application of relational structures presented in the strategy of the classic.

Translation of ideas nevertheless inevitably involves questions of broad cultural differences and how they are perceived. As far as it is relevant to a politically sensitive text like *The Art of War*, to Occidental eyes the distinguishing mark of traditional Chinese social thought in actual practice is authoritarianism, and there is much empirical evidence to support this view of Confucian society. While it is true that personal loyalty, such as would serve for a cement in an authoritarian structure, seems to be esteemed more highly in the social thought of China than in that of the West, nevertheless there is also a broader conception of loyalty to abstractions or ideals that surfaces even in Confucian thought.

In Confucian idealism, a man does not participate in an organization or cause that he does not believe is reasonable and just. Once he truly believes it is right, however, a man should not abandon a course of action even if it brings him hardship and peril. Confucius said that it is a disgrace to be rich and honored in an unjust state, and he himself nearly died for his independence. According to the classics, loyalty does not mean blind obedience to an individual or state, but includes the duty of conscientious protest. Loyalty to ideals above all may be rare in practice, but it always was part of the Chinese worldview.

In the organizational science of *The Art of War*, loyalty is not so much a moral standard in itself but a product of social relations within the organization based on other professional and ethical standards. The quality of the relationship between the leaders and the troops is what

cements loyalty, according to Master Sun, and this is reinforced by egalitarian adherence to established standards of behavior.

There are different ways of interpreting ideals in real life, of course, and there is not necessarily an unambiguous course of action dictated by the general concept of loyalty, when there are various levels of relevance to consider. One of the stories related in commentary on *The Art of War* concerns the whole question of loyalty addressed from different points of view, illustrating the interplay of these different views of an appropriate context for loyalty.

During a war a certain brigadier general had his entire contingent wiped out in battle; he himself fought until the end, then returned to headquarters to report. Now, since there had been some problems with discipline and morale, there was talk of making an example of this general, accusing him of deserting his troops—not dying with them—and putting him to death.

Finally it was objected, however, that he had in fact fought to the last man, after which there was no reason to continue, so he returned for reassignment; thus neither his loyalty to his troops nor his loyalty to his nation could be denied. Furthermore, if he were to be executed, it was argued in his defense, others would not necessarily be cowed into obedience but would more likely become alienated, seeing that there was no reason to return home.

On a level of understanding more sophisticated than that of broad generalizations, one of the most challenging and rewarding uses of classical literature is the exploration of the psychological nuances of basic concepts and their manifestations in practice. It is challenging because it demands immersion in the consciousness of the classics themselves; it is rewarding because it opens up realms of thought beyond predetermined subjective parameters. The key to this appreciation is a sensitivity to structure, traditionally awakened as much by allegory and imagery as by discourse and argument.

The use of imagery and suggestion in Chinese literature was practiced as a fine art in the Chan Buddhism of the Tang and Sung dynasties, which inherited the traditions of the Confucian and Taoist classics as well as those of the Buddhist sutras. Chan Buddhism influenced all the great scholars, artists, and poets of China then and thereafter, yet

Chan was in its turn indebted to classical Taoism for support in the acceptance of its surprising literary devices. One of the linguistic techniques of this fine art that is of particular concern to the translator is the use of ambiguity.

Taoist and Buddhist literature have been described—both by Easterners writing for Westerners and by Westerners writing for other Westerners—as paradoxical, so frequently and to such a degree that paradox is commonly considered one of the major characteristics or devices of this literature. The orientation of *The Art of War* toward winning without fighting, for example, is typical of this sort of paradox, which is there to invite attention to its own logic. It may paradoxically be nonparadoxical, therefore, to find that the paradox of ambiguity is an exact science in the Taoist literature of higher psychology.

The first maneuver of this literature is to engage the participation of the reader in the work, just as the viewer is drawn into the pattern of suggestion spun by lines in space on seeing an expert Sung-dynasty ink line drawing. The result is partly from the writing and partly from the reading; used as a tool for the assessment of the mentality of the reader, each aphorism, each text, brings out a particular facet of human psychology. Chan Buddhists often used ambiguity primarily as a means of nondirective mirroring of personalities and mind sets; *The Art of War* similarly has the power to reveal a great deal about its readers through their reactions and interpretations.

As a translator, therefore, I have always considered the faithful reconstruction of a necessary or useful ambiguity to be among the most difficult subtleties of the craft. Commentators on Chinese classics have long shown how thoroughly different perspectives can be obtained by adopting the different sets of subject or object associations that certain sentences allow. In the later Chan schools, it was openly stated that classic texts were meant to be read by putting yourself in everyone's place to get a comprehensive view of subjective and objective relationships, and the Chan writers took this to breathtakingly distant lengths in an elaborate imagery of transformation and interpenetration of viewpoints.

In a classical aphorism on education frequently encountered in Chan literature, Confucius said, "If I bring up one corner, and those to whom I am speaking cannot come back with the other three, I don't talk to them anymore." Applied to a Chinese classic, this produces a fair description of the experience of reading such a book. Put in a positive way, Confucius said the classics give hints, suggestions that yield more only with time and thought given to applying these hints to present real situations. Similarly, in Taoist tradition they are used as visualization models, designed to awaken certain perceptions of human nature and the human condition.

It is the intention of this translation of *The Art of War*, therefore, to reproduce the classic as a study of relationships, or energy in potential and in motion, that could remain useful through changes in time, linked with the perennial Taoist tradition that marks the heart and soul of this classic text. Comments by the readers mentioned above, written over a period of nearly a thousand years, have been selected not only to elucidate the original text but also to illustrate the shifting of perspectives that the classic makes possible. The translation of the original has therefore been designed to provide conceptual space for different views in specific places.

The reason that classics remain classics over thousands of years, as *The Art of War* has remained along with the works of the original Confucian and Taoist sages, seems to be that they continue to have meaning. This continuing meaning, moreover, is not experienced only over generations. On a small scale, a classic yields significantly different meanings when read in different circumstances and moods; on a larger scale, a classic conveys wholly different worlds when read in different times of life, at different stages of experience, feeling, and understanding of life. Classics may be interesting and even entertaining, but people always find they are not like books used for diversion, which give up all of their content at once; the classics seem to grow wiser as we grow wiser, more useful the more we use them.

THE ART OF WAR

INU SHIN
Thirteenth century,
one of the "Twelve
Heavenly Generals"

STRATEGIC ASSESSMENTS

MILITARY ACTION IS IMPORTANT TO THE NATION—IT IS THE GROUND OF DEATH AND LIFE, THE PATH OF SURVIVAL AND DESTRUCTION, SO IT IS IMPERATIVE TO EXAMINE IT.

MASTER SUN

Military action is inauspicious—it is only considered important because it is a matter of life and death, and there is the possibility that it may be taken up lightly.

LI QUAN

The survival or destruction of a country and the life or death of its people may depend on military action, so it is necessary to examine it carefully.

DU MU

The ground means the location, the place of pitched battle—gain the advantage and you live, lose the advantage and you die. Therefore military action is called the ground of death and life. The path means the way to adjust to the situation and establish victory—find this and you survive, lose this and you perish. Therefore it is said to be imperative to examine it. An ancient document says, "There is a way of survival, which helps and strengthens you; there is a way of destruction, which pushes you into oblivion."

JIA LIN

Whether you live or die depends on the configuration of the battleground; whether you survive or perish depends on the way of battle.

MEI YAOCHEN

MASTER SUN THEREFORE MEASURE IN TERMS OF FIVE THINGS, USE THESE ASSESS-MENTS TO MAKE COMPARISONS, AND THUS FIND OUT WHAT THE CON-DITIONS ARE. THE FIVE THINGS ARE THE WAY, THE WEATHER, THE TERRAIN, THE LEADERSHIP, AND DISCIPLINE.

DU MU

Five things are to be assessed—the way, the weather, the lay of the land, the leadership, and discipline. These are to be assessed at headquarters—first assess yourself and your opponent in terms of these five things, deciding who is superior. Then you can determine who is likely to prevail. Having determined this, only then should you mobilize your forces.

CAO CAO

Assessments of the following items are to be made at headquarters: the leadership, the opponent, the terrain, troop strength, distance, and relative danger.

WANG XI

Assess the leadership, the environmental conditions, discipline, troops, officers, and the system of rewards and punishments.

ZHANG YU

Master Guan said that assessments should be made at home before sending troops abroad. Assessments are the first order of business in military operations. Some say that military operations should be adjusted right on the spot, in confrontation with the opponent, but General Cao Cao says that assessments should be made at headquarters—this is because it is imperative first to assess the wisdom of the leaders, the strength of the opponent, the lay of the land, and the number of troops; then when the two armies confront one another, the adaptations to be made are determined by the leadership in a manner consistent with these calculations.

Discipline means that regulations are strict and clear. The reason that leadership and discipline come last in this list of five things is that whenever you mobilize to attack those who have done you wrong, it is necessary first to look into the matter of whether you are appreciated and trusted by your own people, then to assess the favorability or otherwise of weather conditions, and then examine the qualities of the terrain. Once these three things are fulfilled, then a leader is appointed to go forth on the expedition. Once the army has gone forth, all orders come from the general.

WANG XI

Harmony among people is the basis of the Way of military operations; the right weather and an advantageous position help. When these three elements are present, then is the time to discuss mobilizing the army. Mobilizing the army requires ability on the part of the leadership. When the leadership is able, then there will be good discipline.

MASTER SUN

THE WAY MEANS INDUCING THE PEOPLE TO HAVE THE SAME AIM AS THE LEADERSHIP, SO THAT THEY WILL SHARE DEATH AND SHARE LIFE, WITHOUT FEAR OF DANGER.

CAO CAO

This means guiding them by instruction and direction. Danger means distrust.

ZHANG YU

If the people are treated with benevolence, faithfulness, and justice, then they will be of one mind, and will be glad to serve. The *I Ching* says, "Joyful in difficulty, the people forget about their death."

DU MU

The Way means humaneness and justice. In ancient times a famous minister of state asked a political philosopher about military matters. The philosopher said, "Humaneness and justice are the means by which to govern properly. When government is carried out properly, people feel close to the leadership and think little of dying for it."

JIA LIN

If the leaders can be humane and just, sharing both the gains and the troubles of the people, then the troops will be loyal and naturally identify with the interests of the leadership.

MASTER SUN

THE WEATHER MEANS THE SEASONS.

CAO CAO

The rules of the ancient military state that operations should not be carried out in winter or summer, out of concern for the people.

ZHANG YU

(*Quoting the founder of the Tang Dynasty*)
In ancient times many soldiers lost their fingers to frostbite on campaigns against the Huns, and many soldiers died of plague on campaigns against the southern tribes. This was because of carrying out operations in winter and summer.

(*Quoting Fan Li*)
This is the meaning of the saying, "Don't go into another's territory at an unfavorable time."

MASTER SUN

THE TERRAIN IS TO BE ASSESSED IN TERMS OF DISTANCE, DIFFICULTY OR EASE OF TRAVEL, DIMENSION, AND SAFETY.

ZHANG YU

In any military operation, it is important first to know the lay of the land. When you know the distance to be traveled, then you can plan whether to proceed directly or by a circuitous route. When you know the difficulty or ease of travel, then you can determine the advantages of infantry or mounted troops. When you know the dimensions of the area, then you can assess how many troops you need, many or few. When you know the relative safety of the terrain, then you can discern whether to do battle or disperse.

MASTER SUN

LEADERSHIP IS A MATTER OF INTELLIGENCE, TRUSTWORTHINESS, HUMANENESS, COURAGE, AND STERNNESS.

CAO CAO

A general should have these five virtues.

DU MU

The Way of the ancient kings was to consider humaneness foremost, while the martial artists considered intelligence foremost. This is because intelligence involves ability to plan and to know when to change effectively. Trustworthiness means to make people sure of punishment or reward. Humaneness means love and compassion for people, being aware of their toils. Courage means to seize opportunities to make certain of victory, without vacillation. Sternness means to establish discipline in the ranks by strict punishments.

JIA LIN

Reliance on intelligence alone results in rebelliousness. Exercise of humaneness alone results in weakness. Fixation on trust results in folly. Dependence on the strength of courage results in violence. Excessive sternness of command results in cruelty. When one has all five virtues together, each appropriate to its function, then one can be a military leader.

MASTER SUN	DISCIPLINE MEANS ORGANIZATION, CHAIN OF COMMAND, AND LOGISTICS.
MEI YAOCHEN	Organization means that the troops must be grouped in a regulated manner. Chain of command means that there must be officers to keep the troops together and lead them. Logistics means overseeing supplies.
MASTER SUN	EVERY GENERAL HAS HEARD OF THESE FIVE THINGS. THOSE WHO KNOW THEM PREVAIL, THOSE WHO DO NOT KNOW THEM DO NOT PREVAIL.
ZHANG YU	Everyone has heard of these five things, but only those who deeply understand the principles of adaptation and impasse will win.
MASTER SUN	THEREFORE USE THESE ASSESSMENTS FOR COMPARISON, TO FIND OUT WHAT THE CONDITIONS ARE. THAT IS TO SAY, WHICH POLITICAL LEADERSHIP HAS THE WAY? WHICH GENERAL HAS ABILITY? WHO HAS THE BETTER CLIMATE AND TERRAIN? WHOSE DISCIPLINE IS EFFECTIVE? WHOSE TROOPS ARE THE STRONGER? WHOSE OFFICERS AND SOLDIERS ARE THE BETTER TRAINED? WHOSE SYSTEM OF REWARDS AND PUNISHMENTS IS CLEARER? THIS IS HOW YOU CAN KNOW WHO WILL WIN.
LI QUAN	A political leadership that has the Way will surely have a military leadership that has intelligence and ability.
DU MU	Ask yourself which political leadership—your own or that of your enemy—is able to reject flatterers and draw close to the wise.
DU YOU	The Way means virtue. It is first necessary to compare the political leadership of nations at war.
MEI YAOCHEN	The question regarding political leadership is, who is able to win the hearts of the people.
HO YANXI	The ancient classic of documents says, "The one who treats me well is

my leader, the one who treats me cruelly is my enemy." The question is, which side has a humane government, and which side has a cruel government.

First compare the political leadership of the two nations at war, in terms of which one has the Way of benevolence and good faith. Then examine the military leadership—who has intelligence, trustworthiness, humaneness, bravery, and sternness. Now observe which side has the environmental advantages.

ZHANG YU

Set up rules that are not to be broken, do not fail to punish any offenders.

CAO CAO

When it comes to establishing rules and regulations, everyone, high and low, should be treated alike.

DU MU

Compare whose orders are the more effective—whose subordinates do not dare to disobey.

DU YOU

Make everyone equal under the law.

MEI YAOCHEN

See who is able to make rules clear and commands easy to follow, so that people listen and obey.

WANG XI

(*On the matters of strength and training*)
When superior and subordinate are in harmony, equally brave in battle, that makes for strength.

DU MU

Know whose armaments are more effective, and whose troops are carefully chosen and well trained. As it is said, "If soldiers do not practice day to day, on the front lines they will be fearful and hesitant. If generals do not practice day to day, on the front lines they will not know how to adapt."

DU YOU

(*Turning to the subject of punishments and rewards*)
Rewards should not be out of proportion, punishments should not be arbitrary.

DU MU

BRONZE SWORD
Fourth century B.C.E.
Photograph courtesy of
Eskenazi Limited, London

Know whose system of rewards for the good and punishments for the bad is clearly defined. As it is said, "If rewards are immoderate, there will be expenditure that does not result in gratitude; if punishments are immoderate, there will be slaughter that does not result in awe."

DU YOU

When people deserve reward, this should be duly noted even if you personally detest them. When people deserve punishment, this should not be forgone even if they are close to you.

MEI YAOCHEN

(*Summing up*)
By assessing these seven things you can know who will be victorious and who will be defeated.

CAO CAO

If you can find out the real conditions, then you will know who will prevail.

MEI YAOCHEN

If you are superior in all of these seven things, you have won before you have even done battle. If you are inferior in all of these seven things, you have lost even before you go into battle. Therefore it is possible to know the victor beforehand.

ZHANG YU

ASSESS THE ADVANTAGES IN TAKING ADVICE, THEN STRUCTURE YOUR FORCES ACCORDINGLY, TO SUPPLEMENT EXTRAORDINARY TACTICS. FORCES ARE TO BE STRUCTURED STRATEGICALLY, BASED ON WHAT IS ADVANTAGEOUS.

MASTER SUN

Structure depends on strategy; strategy is determined according to events.

CAO CAO

A MILITARY OPERATION INVOLVES DECEPTION. EVEN THOUGH YOU ARE COMPETENT, APPEAR TO BE INCOMPETENT. THOUGH EFFECTIVE, APPEAR TO BE INEFFECTIVE.

MASTER SUN

A military operation has no standard form—it goes by way of deception.

CAO CAO

Without deception you cannot carry out strategy, without strategy you cannot control the opponent.

MEI YAOCHEN

WANG XI | Deception is for the purpose of seeking victory over an enemy; to command a group requires truthfulness.

ZHANG YU | While strong in reality, appear to be weak; while brave in reality, appear to be cowardly—this method was effective against the Huns.

LI QUAN | Li Quan told a story of how one of the generals of the Han dynasty rebelled and joined forces with the Huns. The emperor sent ten scouts to observe them, and all reported that they could be effectively attacked. The emperor then sent one Lou Jing, who reported that, on the contrary, the Huns could not be effectively attacked. When the emperor asked him why, he replied, "When two countries are at a standoff, they should be flaunting their strengths. When I went, all I saw were the feeble and the elderly—surely they are 'competent yet appearing to be incompetent,' so I consider it unfeasible to attack."

The emperor was wroth. He punished Lou Jing for getting in his way, and personally set out with a large contingent. They were hemmed in by the Huns, however, and cut off from supplies for seven days.

This, concluded Li, is the meaning of an army appearing to be weak.

DU MU | This is a matter of deceptively concealing your state. You should not let the opponent see what state you are in, for if the enemy sees your condition, he will surely have a response. An example of this is when the Huns let the emissaries of Han only see the feeble and the old.

DU YOU | This means that when you are really competent and effective you outwardly appear to be incompetent and ineffective, so as to cause the enemy to be unprepared.

WANG XI | When strong, appear weak. Brave, appear fearful. Orderly, appear chaotic. Full, appear empty. Wise, appear foolish. Many, appear to be few. Advancing, appear to retreat. Moving quickly, appear to be slow. Taking, appear to leave. In one place, appear to be in another.

ZHANG YU | When you are going to do battle, make it seem as if you are retreating. When you are going to hasten, make it seem as if you are relaxing.

WHEN YOU ARE GOING TO ATTACK NEARBY, MAKE IT LOOK AS IF YOU ARE GOING TO GO A LONG WAY; WHEN YOU ARE GOING TO ATTACK FAR AWAY, MAKE IT LOOK AS IF YOU ARE GOING JUST A SHORT DISTANCE.

MASTER SUN

This is to cause the opponent to be unprepared.

LI QUAN

DRAW THEM IN WITH THE PROSPECT OF GAIN, TAKE THEM BY CONFUSION.

MASTER SUN

If they are greedy, lure them with goods.

MEI YAOCHEN

Show them a little prospect of gain to lure them, then attack and overcome them.

ZHANG YU

When the enemy is confused, you can use this opportunity to take them.

DU MU

I would have crafty interlopers confuse them, then wait for them to fall into disarray in order to take them.

JIA LIN

Use deception to throw them into confusion, lead them on in order to take them. When the states of Wu and Yue were at war with each other, Wu sent out three thousand criminals to give an appearance of disorder so as to lure Yue. Some of the criminals ran, some of them gave up; the Yue army fought with them, only to be defeated by the army of Wu.

ZHANG YU

WHEN THEY ARE FULFILLED, BE PREPARED AGAINST THEM; WHEN THEY ARE STRONG, AVOID THEM.

MASTER SUN

If the enemy's government is fulfilled—meaning that there is mutual love between the rulers and the ruled, there is clarity and trustworthiness in the system of rewards and punishments, and the soldiers are well trained—then you should be on guard against them. Do not wait for a clash to make your preparations. When the enemy's military is strong,

DU MU

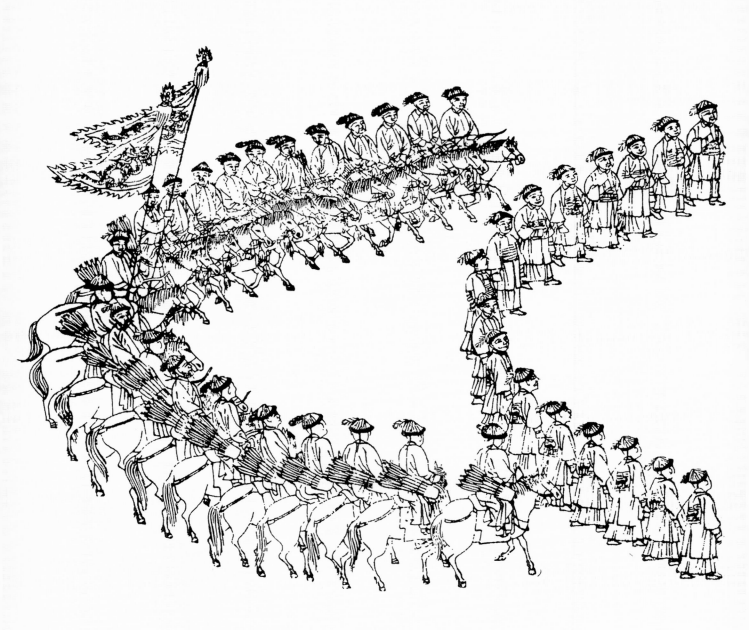

CAVALRY AND FOOT SOLDIERS
Ch'ing dynasty, 1644–1911

you should avoid them for the time being, waiting until they slack off, watching for an opening to attack.

If the enemy does not stir, is complete and fulfilled, then you should prepare carefully. Fulfill yourself too, so as to be ready for them.

CHEN HAO

If you only see fulfillment in the enemy, and do not see any gap, then you should build up your power to be prepared.

HO YANXI

A classic says, "Struggling with them, you find out where they have plenty and where they are lacking." Having plenty is what is meant by being fulfilled, lacking is what is meant by having gaps. Once the military power of the adversary is full, you should treat them as if they were unbeatable, and not attack lightly. As a military guide says, "When you see a gap, then advance; when you see fullness, then stop."

ZHANG YU

For the weak to control the strong, it is logically necessary to await a change.

JIA LIN

When their storehouses are full and their soldiers are in top form, then you should withdraw in order to watch for an opening when they relax, observing any changes and responding to them.

DU YOU

USE ANGER TO THROW THEM INTO DISARRAY.

MASTER SUN

Wait for them to become decadent and lazy.

CAO CAO

When the military leadership is often angered, its strategy is easily thrown into confusion, for its nature is unstable.

LI QUAN

When their military leadership is obstreperous, you should irritate them to make them angry—then they will become impetuous and ignore their original strategy.

DU MU

If they are quick-tempered, then stir them up to excite them so that they go into battle carelessly.

MEI YAOCHEN

ZHANG YU	If they are violent and easily angered, then use embarrassment to enrage them, so that their morale is upset—then they will proceed carelessly, without formulating a plan.
MASTER SUN	USE HUMILITY TO MAKE THEM HAUGHTY.
LI QUAN	If they ply you with expensive gifts and sweet talk, they are up to something.
DU YOU	When they are stirred up and about to make their move, then you should pretend to be cowed, so as to raise their spirits; wait for them to slack off, then regroup and attack.
MEI YAOCHEN	Give the appearance of inferiority and weakness, to make them proud.
WANG XI	Appear to be lowly and weak, so as to make them arrogant—then they will not worry about you, and you can attack them as they relax.
MASTER SUN	TIRE THEM BY FLIGHT.
CAO CAO	Use swiftness to wear them out.
WANG XI	This means making a lot of surprise attacks. When they come out, you go home; when they go home, you go out. When they go to the aid of their left flank, you head to the right; when they go to the aid of their right flank, you go to the left. This way you can tire them out.
ZHANG YU	This way, your strength will remain intact, while they will be worn out.
MASTER SUN	CAUSE DIVISION AMONG THEM.
CAO CAO	Send interlopers to cause rifts among them.
LI QUAN	Break up their accords, cause division between the leadership and their ministers, and then attack.

INFANTRY OFFICER
Ch'in dynasty,
221—206 B.C.E.

DU MU   This means that if there are good relations between the enemy leadership and its followers, then you should use bribes to cause division.

CHEN HAO   If they are stingy, you be generous; if they are harsh, you be lenient.
That way their leadership and followers will be suspicious of each other,
and you can cause division between them.

DU YOU   Seduce them with the prospect of gain, send interlopers in among them,
have rhetoricians use fast talk to ingratiate themselves with their leaders
and followers, and divide up their organization and power.

ZHANG YU   You may cause rifts between the leadership and their followers, or between them and their allies—cause division, and then take aim at them.

MASTER SUN   ATTACK WHEN THEY ARE UNPREPARED, MAKE YOUR MOVE WHEN
THEY DO NOT EXPECT IT.

CAO CAO   Attack when they are slacking off, make your move when a gap opens
up.

MENG SHI   Strike at their gaps, attack when they are lax, don't let the enemy figure
out how to prepare. This is why it is said that in military operations
formlessness is the most effective. One of the great warrior-leaders said,
"The most efficient of movements is the one that is unexpected; the best
of plans is the one that is unknown."

MASTER SUN   THE FORMATION AND PROCEDURE USED BY THE MILITARY SHOULD
NOT BE DIVULGED BEFOREHAND.

CAO CAO   To divulge means to leak out. The military has no constant form, just
as water has no constant shape—adapt as you face the enemy, without
letting them know beforehand what you are going to do. Therefore, assessment of the enemy is in the mind, observation of the situation is in
the eyes.

LI QUAN   Attack when they are unprepared and not expecting it, and you will surely win. This is the essence of martial arts, to be kept secret and not divulged.

To divulge something means to speak of it. This means that all of the aforementioned strategies for securing military victory can certainly not be made uniform—first, see the enemy's formation, and only then apply them. You cannot say what you will do before the event.

DU MU

Since you adapt and adjust appropriately in face of the enemy, how could you say what you are going to do beforehand?

MEI YAOCHEN

THE ONE WHO FIGURES ON VICTORY AT HEADQUARTERS BEFORE EVEN DOING BATTLE IS THE ONE WHO HAS THE MOST STRATEGIC FACTORS ON HIS SIDE. THE ONE WHO FIGURES ON INABILITY TO PREVAIL AT HEADQUARTERS BEFORE DOING BATTLE IS THE ONE WHO HAS THE LEAST STRATEGIC FACTORS ON HIS SIDE. THE ONE WITH MANY STRATEGIC FACTORS IN HIS FAVOR WINS, THE ONE WITH FEW STRATEGIC FACTORS IN HIS FAVOR LOSES—HOW MUCH THE MORE SO FOR ONE WITH NO STRATEGIC FACTORS IN HIS FAVOR. OBSERVING THE MATTER IN THIS WAY, I CAN SEE WHO WILL WIN AND WHO WILL LOSE.

MASTER SUN

When your strategy is deep and far-reaching, then what you gain by your calculations is much, so you can win before you even fight. When your strategic thinking is shallow and near-sighted, then what you gain by your calculations is little, so you lose before you do battle. Much strategy prevails over little strategy, so those with no strategy cannot but be defeated. Therefore it is said that victorious warriors win first and then go to war, while defeated warriors go to war first and then seek to win.

ZHANG YU

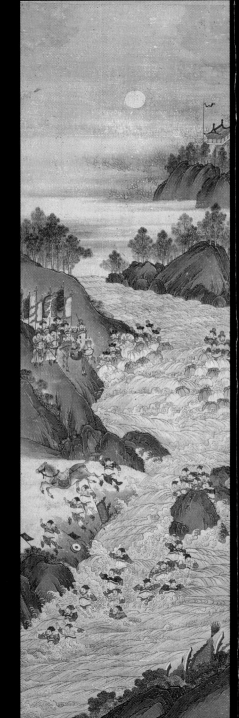

DOING BATTLE

First establish your plans, then prepare your equipment. This is why the chapter on battle follows the chapter on strategic assessments.

LI QUAN

WHEN YOU DO BATTLE, EVEN IF YOU ARE WINNING, IF YOU CON-TINUE FOR A LONG TIME IT WILL DULL YOUR FORCES AND BLUNT YOUR EDGE; IF YOU BESIEGE A CITADEL, YOUR STRENGTH WILL BE EX-HAUSTED. IF YOU KEEP YOUR ARMIES OUT IN THE FIELD FOR A LONG TIME, YOUR SUPPLIES WILL BE INSUFFICIENT.

MASTER SUN

Even if you prevail over others in battle, if you go on too long there will be no profit. In military operations, total victory is important; if you dull your forces and blunt your edge, sustaining casualties and battle fatigue, then you will be exhausted.

JIA LIN

When you are spending a great deal of money on a military operation, if the army is out in the field too long, your budget will not be enough to cover the expense.

ZHANG YU

As the classic *Spring and Autumn Annals* says, "War is like a fire—if you do not put it out, it will burn itself out."

LI QUAN

If a military operation goes on for a long time without accomplishing anything, your rivals will begin to get ideas.

JIA LIN

DU YOU	Arms are tools of ill omen—to employ them for an extended period of time will bring about calamity. As it is said, "Those who like to fight and so exhaust their military inevitably perish."
MASTER SUN	WHEN YOUR FORCES ARE DULLED, YOUR EDGE IS BLUNTED, YOUR STRENGTH IS EXHAUSTED, AND YOUR SUPPLIES ARE GONE, THEN OTHERS WILL TAKE ADVANTAGE OF YOUR DEBILITY AND RISE UP. THEN EVEN IF YOU HAVE WISE ADVISERS YOU CANNOT MAKE THINGS TURN OUT WELL IN THE END.
LI QUAN	A large-scale operation involves enormous expense, which not only breaks you down in the field, but also exhausts you at home. Therefore a wise government does not keep its army in the field.
MASTER SUN	THEREFORE I HAVE HEARD OF MILITARY OPERATIONS THAT WERE CLUMSY BUT SWIFT, BUT I HAVE NEVER SEEN ONE THAT WAS SKILLFUL AND LASTED A LONG TIME. IT IS NEVER BENEFICIAL TO A NATION TO HAVE A MILITARY OPERATION CONTINUE FOR A LONG TIME.
CAO CAO	Some win through speed, even if they are clumsy.
DU MU	Some may be clumsy in attack, but they get the upper hand through extraordinary swiftness, because they are not subject to the problems of wearing out their forces and using up their resources.
CHEN HAO	As it is said, be swift as the thunder that peals before you have a chance to cover your ears, fast as the lightning that flashes before you can blink your eyes.
MASTER SUN	THEREFORE, THOSE WHO ARE NOT THOROUGHLY AWARE OF THE DISADVANTAGES IN THE USE OF ARMS CANNOT BE THOROUGHLY AWARE OF THE ADVANTAGES IN THE USE OF ARMS.
LI QUAN	Advantages and disadvantages are interdependent—first know the disadvantages, then you know the advantages.

JIA LIN	When the generals are haughty and the soldiers are lazy, in their greed for gain they forget that there may be an unexpected turn of events—this is the greatest disadvantage.
DU YOU	This means that if you are planning to mobilize your forces and embark upon a campaign, if you do not first think about the calamities of danger and destruction, you will not be able to reap any advantage.
MASTER SUN	THOSE WHO USE THE MILITARY SKILLFULLY DO NOT RAISE TROOPS TWICE AND DO NOT PROVIDE FOOD THREE TIMES.
CAO CAO	This means you draft people into service once and then immediately seize victory—you do not go back to your country a second time to raise more troops. At first you provide food, after that you feed off the enemy; and then when your soldiers return to your country, you do not greet them with yet more free food.
DU MU	Determine whether the enemy can be successfully attacked, determine whether you can do battle, and only afterward raise troops—then you can overcome the enemy and return home.
LI QUAN	Do not raise troops twice, lest the citizenry become wearied and bitterness arise.
MASTER SUN	BY TAKING EQUIPMENT FROM YOUR OWN COUNTRY BUT FEEDING OFF THE ENEMY YOU CAN BE SUFFICIENT IN BOTH ARMS AND PROVISIONS.
CAO CAO	When you are going to go to war, first you must calculate your expenses, and strive to feed off the opponent.
LI QUAN	If you have your own arms and take food from the enemy, then even if the campaign takes you far afield you will not lack for anything.
CAO CAO	Armaments are taken from the homeland, provisions are taken from the enemy.

WHEN A COUNTRY IS IMPOVERISHED BY MILITARY OPERATIONS, IT IS BECAUSE OF TRANSPORTING SUPPLIES TO A DISTANT PLACE. TRANSPORT SUPPLIES TO A DISTANT PLACE, AND THE POPULACE WILL BE IMPOVERISHED.

Troops are raised repeatedly, and the levies are heavy.

Master Guan said, "When provisions go for three hundred miles, the country is out a year's supplies; when provisions go for four hundred miles, the country is out two years' supplies; when provisions go for five hundred miles, the people pale with hunger." This means that food should not be transported, for if it is, the producers will lose, so they cannot be impoverished.

Transporting supplies to distant places means that wealth is expended in travel and used up on transportation, so that the common people become poorer day by day.

When seven hundred thousand families have to support an army of one hundred thousand on a distant expedition, the common peoples cannot avoid impoverishment.

THOSE WHO ARE NEAR THE ARMY SELL AT HIGH PRICES. BECAUSE OF HIGH PRICES, THE WEALTH OF THE COMMON PEOPLE IS EXHAUSTED.

When the army has gone forth, those who are near the troops, greedy for money, sell at high prices. Therefore the common people become destitute.

Near the army there is always trade; the common people use up their wealth to go along with it, and so become destitute.

Wherever the troops gather, the prices of goods all soar. Since people are greedy for exceptional profits, they sell off all their goods. Though at first they make a great deal of profit, in the end they run out of goods. Also, since there are extraordinary levies, those with something

BATTLE SCENE FROM THE TAIPING REBELLION
Ch'ing dynasty, 1644–1911
Cemec Ltd, courtesy of Sydney L. Moss Ltd, London

to sell demand the highest prices they can get; the common people go broke trying to buy things, so the country naturally is impoverished.

WANG XI

When supplies are transported far away, the people are worn out by the expense. In the markets near the army, the prices of goods shoot up. Therefore long military campaigns are a plague to a nation.

MASTER SUN

WHEN RESOURCES ARE EXHAUSTED, THEN LEVIES ARE MADE UNDER PRESSURE. WHEN POWER AND RESOURCES ARE EXHAUSTED, THEN THE HOMELAND IS DRAINED. THE COMMON PEOPLE ARE DEPRIVED OF SEVENTY PERCENT OF THEIR BUDGET, WHILE THE GOVERNMENT'S EXPENSES FOR EQUIPMENT AMOUNT TO SIXTY PERCENT OF ITS BUDGET.

DU MU

If the military situation is not resolved and the army is not demobilized, levies become increasingly oppressive, resulting in exhaustion of the resources of the people, so that they lose most of what they produce.

HO YANXI

The people are the basis of a country, food is the heaven of the people. Those who rule over others should respect this and be sparing.

MEI YAOCHEN

The common people provide goods, food, and labor for the use of the military, thus losing most of their own sustenance, while the government provides equipment for the use of the military, thus losing more than half of its budget. Therefore taxes are used up, the army is worn out, and the populace is exhausted. When levies are oppressive and the people are impoverished, the country is drained.

MASTER SUN

THEREFORE A WISE GENERAL STRIVES TO FEED OFF THE ENEMY. EACH POUND OF FOOD TAKEN FROM THE ENEMY IS EQUIVALENT TO TWENTY POUNDS YOU PROVIDE BY YOURSELF.

CAO CAO

Transportation of provisions itself consumes twenty times the amount transported.

ZHANG YU

It takes twenty pounds of provisions to deliver one pound of provisions to a distant army. If the terrain is rugged, it takes even more than that. That is why an able general will always feed off the enemy.

SO WHAT KILLS THE ENEMY IS ANGER, WHAT GETS THE ENEMY'S GOODS IS REWARD.
MASTER SUN

If you stir up your officers and troops so that they are all enraged, then they will kill the enemy. If you reward your men with spoils, that will make them fight on their own initiative, so the enemy's goods can be taken. That is why it is said that where there are big rewards there are valiant men.
ZHANG YU

If people know they will be richly rewarded if they overcome the opponent, then they will gladly go into battle.
DU YOU

This just means establishing rich rewards—if you let the troops plunder at will, they may get out of hand.
WANG XI

THEREFORE, IN A CHARIOT BATTLE, REWARD THE FIRST TO CAPTURE AT LEAST TEN CHARIOTS.
MASTER SUN

If you reward everyone, there will not be enough to go around, so you offer a reward to one in order to encourage everyone.
MEI YAOCHEN

CHANGE THEIR COLORS, USE THEM MIXED IN WITH YOUR OWN. TREAT THE SOLDIERS WELL, TAKE CARE OF THEM.
MASTER SUN

You change their colors to make them the same as your own, you use them mixed in with your own so as not to leave them to their own devices.
CAO CAO

You change their colors so that they won't be recognizable to the enemy.
JIA LIN

Captured soldiers should be well treated, to get them to work for you.
ZHANG YU

THIS IS CALLED OVERCOMING THE OPPONENT AND INCREASING YOUR STRENGTH TO BOOT.
MASTER SUN

HORSE AND CHARIOT. First century C.E. China.
Courtesy of R. H. Ellsworth, Ltd

By capturing the opponent's soldiers and using the enemy's supplies, you increase your own strength.

DU MU

When you capture soldiers, give them responsibilities according to their strengths, take care of them kindly, and they will work for you.

MEI YAOCHEN

If you use the enemy to defeat the enemy, you will be strong wherever you go.

HO YANXI

SO THE IMPORTANT THING IN A MILITARY OPERATION IS VICTORY, NOT PERSISTENCE.

MASTER SUN

Persistence is not profitable. An army is like fire—if you don't put it out, it will burn itself out.

CAO CAO

What is best is a quick victory and a speedy return.

MENG SHI

In all of the above-mentioned, it is important to be quick. If you are quick, then you can economize on expenditures and allow the people rest.

MEI YAOCHEN

HENCE, WE KNOW THAT THE LEADER OF THE ARMY IS IN CHARGE OF THE LIVES OF THE PEOPLE AND THE SAFETY OF THE NATION.

MASTER SUN

If the military leadership is wise, the country is safe.

CAO CAO

This tells us how serious the matter of appointing military leaders is.

MEI YAOCHEN

The lives of the people and the order of the nation are in the charge of the generals. The difficulty of finding good leadership material is a perennial problem.

WANG XI

WARRIOR
Tang dynasty,
618-907 C.E.

THREE

PLANNING A SIEGE

THE GENERAL RULE FOR USE OF THE MILITARY IS THAT IT IS BETTER TO KEEP A NATION INTACT THAN TO DESTROY IT. IT IS BETTER TO KEEP AN ARMY INTACT THAN TO DESTROY IT, BETTER TO KEEP A DIVISION INTACT THAN TO DESTROY IT, BETTER TO KEEP A BATTALION INTACT THAN TO DESTROY IT, BETTER TO KEEP A UNIT INTACT THAN TO DESTROY IT.

MASTER SUN

If you raise an army and penetrate deeply into your opponent's territory, keeping on the move, blocking the space between the inner stronghold and the outer city walls, cutting off communications between inside and outside, then if the opponent surrenders completely, that is best. If you attack destructively and take a nation by force, that is a lesser accomplishment.

CAO CAO

If you can keep the opponent's nation intact, then your own nation will also be intact. So this is best.

JIA LIN

This means that killing is not the important thing.

LI QUAN

It is best if an enemy nation comes and surrenders of its own accord. To attack and defeat it is inferior to this.

DU YOU

The best policy is to use strategy, influence, and the trend of events to cause the adversary to submit willingly.

HO YANXI

ZHANG YU	Zhang Yu quoted a statement by Wei Liaozi: "Practicing martial arts, assess your opponents; cause them to lose spirit and direction so that even if the opposing army is intact it is useless—this is winning by the Tao. If you destroy the opposing army and kill the generals, mount the ramparts shooting, gather a mob and usurp the land, this is winning by force."
	Zhang Yu then explained, "So winning by the Tao and winning by force mean the same as keeping a nation intact and destroying a nation. Treating the people mercifully while punishing criminals, gaining complete victory with the country intact, is best."
WANG XI	Nation, army, division, battalion, unit—great or small, keep it intact and your dignity will be improved thereby; destroy it, and your dignity will suffer.
MASTER SUN	THEREFORE THOSE WHO WIN EVERY BATTLE ARE NOT REALLY SKILLFUL—THOSE WHO RENDER OTHERS' ARMIES HELPLESS WITHOUT FIGHTING ARE THE BEST OF ALL.
CAO CAO	The best victory is when the opponent surrenders of its own accord before there are any actual hostilities.
LI QUAN	Overcome your opponent by calculation.
CHEN HAO	When you do battle, it is necessary to kill people, so it is best to win without fighting.
JIA LIN	Best of all is when your troops are held in such awe that everyone comes to surrender. This is preferable to winning by trickery, violence, and slaughter.
MEI YAOCHEN	This is a matter of disliking to inflict injury.
ZHANG YU	If you can only prevail after doing battle, there will surely be many casualties, so this is not good. If you make it clear what is to be rewarded and what punished, make your directives reliable, keep your machines in good repair, train and exercise your officers and troops, and let their

strengths be known so as to overcome the opponent psychologically, this is considered very good.

In military operations, what is valued is foiling the opponent's strategy, not pitched battle.   WANG XI

Ho Yanxi related this story: When Wang Po of the latter Han dynasty struck Chu Chien and Su Mo, he returned to camp after battle. His enemies regrouped and tried to provoke another skirmish, but Wang Po refused to come out.   HO YANXI

    As Wang Po was having a dinner party with his officers, Su Mo's men showered the camp with a rain of arrows. One of them even struck the wine keg in front of Wang Po. Wang Po, however, sat there calmly, not stirring a bit.

    At that point an officer remarked that Su Mo was already at the end of his rope and would be easy to strike. Wang Po refused, saying, "Su Mo's mercenaries are from far away, and they are short on supplies—that is why they are trying to pick a winner-take-all fight. If I close off my camp and keep my soldiers in, this is what is called 'best of all.'"

THEREFORE THE SUPERIOR MILITARIST STRIKES WHILE SCHEMES ARE BEING LAID.   MASTER SUN

When the opponent is just beginning to plan its strategy, it is easy to strike.   CAO CAO

Just when the opponent is setting up a plan to mobilize its forces, if your army strikes and suppresses them, that is best. Therefore one of the great warrior-emperors said, "Those who are good at getting rid of trouble are those who take care of it before it arises; those who are good at overcoming opponents are those who win before there is form."   DU YOU

This means winning by intelligence.   MEI YAOCHEN

It is best to thwart people by intelligent planning.   WANG XI

HO YANXI	When the enemy begins to plot an attack against you, you first attack them—this is easy. Figure out the direction of the enemy's plans and deploy your forces accordingly, attacking at the outset of their intentions.
ZHANG YU	Zhang Yu noted that some say that what Master Sun was saying here was that the best military operation is to attack strategically, meaning to use unusual tactics and secret calculations to seize victory without even battling.
MASTER SUN	THE NEXT BEST IS TO ATTACK ALLIANCES.
LI QUAN	This means attacking when alliances are first established.
CHEN HAO	Some say this means that when the enemy has already mobilized and is negotiating, strike and overcome them—this is next best.
MENG SHI	If you carry on alliances with strong countries, your enemies won't dare to plot against you.
MEI YAOCHEN	This means winning by intimidation.
WANG XI	It means if you cannot completely thwart the schemes of the enemy, you should then work on his alliances, to try to make them fall apart.
HO YANXI	What Master Sun said was to attack when you come in contact with the enemy, meaning that when your forces are about to clash, you set up a dummy force to scare them and make them unable either to advance or retreat, and then take advantage of that opportunity to come up and conquer them. Since the neighbors have also been helped by this action of yours, the enemy cannot but be isolated and weak.
MASTER SUN	THE NEXT BEST IS TO ATTACK THE ARMY.
CAO CAO	This means when the army is already formed.

EMPEROR KANGXI. Kangxi period, 1662-1722

JIA LIN	To be good at successful attack, deploying your forces without a hitch, is yet another notch down. Therefore a great warrior-emperor said, "One who fights for victory in front of bared blades is not a good general."
MEI YAOCHEN	This means winning by fighting.
MASTER SUN	THE LOWEST IS TO ATTACK A CITY. SIEGE OF A CITY IS ONLY DONE AS A LAST RESORT.
CAO CAO	When the enemy has called in its resources and is defending a city, to attack them in this condition is the lowest form of military operation.
LI QUAN	When you garrison an army in a walled city, the officers get stale and the soldiers get lazy.
DU YOU	This means that when you attack cities and butcher towns, this is the lowest form of attack, because there are many casualties.
WANG XI	Soldiers are killed and maimed without necessarily taking over the city.
ZHANG YU	The siege of cities and butchering of towns not only ages the army and wastes resources, it also has a lot of casualties, so it is the lowest form of attack. When you besiege a city, then your power will be used up in that, so you do it only if it is absolutely necessary, as a last resort.
MASTER SUN	TAKE THREE MONTHS TO PREPARE YOUR MACHINES AND THREE MONTHS TO COMPLETE YOUR SIEGE ENGINEERING.
DU MU	He means that it is necessary to take time to really prepare machines and constructions thoroughly, lest many people be injured. As one of the ancient strategists said, "Those who cannot deploy their machines effectively are in trouble."
MEI YAOCHEN	If neither intimidation nor intelligence are sufficient to overcome people, and you have no choice but to attack them where they live, then you must take adequate time to prepare.

Some say that Master Sun's point here is that you shouldn't get angry and rush to attack. This is why he says to take time, not because there is necessarily a specific time.

ZHANG YU

IF THE GENERAL CANNOT OVERCOME HIS ANGER AND HAS HIS ARMY SWARM OVER THE CITADEL, KILLING A THIRD OF HIS SOLDIERS, AND YET THE CITADEL IS STILL NOT TAKEN, THIS IS A DISASTROUS ATTACK.

MASTER SUN

If the general is so enraged that he cannot wait for the siege machines, and he sends his soldiers over the walls like a swarm of ants, this is killing and maiming the soldiers.

CAO CAO

Just ingratiate yourself with the people while causing inward rifts among the military, and the city will conquer itself.

JIA LIN

THEREFORE ONE WHO IS GOOD AT MARTIAL ARTS OVERCOMES OTH-ERS' FORCES WITHOUT BATTLE, CONQUERS OTHERS' CITIES WITHOUT SIEGE, DESTROYS OTHERS' NATIONS WITHOUT TAKING A LONG TIME.

MASTER SUN

Use tactics to overcome opponents by dispiriting them rather than by battling with them; take their cities by strategy. Destroy their countries artfully, do not die in protracted warfare.

LI QUAN

Battle means hurting people, siege means destroying things.

MEI YAOCHEN

This means attacking at the planning and attacking the alliances, so as not to come to the point of actually doing battle. This is why classical martial arts say that the best of strategists does not fight. One who is good at laying siege does not lay siege with an army, but uses strategy to thwart the opponents, causing them to overcome themselves and destroy themselves, rather than taking them by a long and troublesome campaign.

HO YANXI

A skillful martialist ruins plans, spoils relations, cuts off supplies, or blocks the way, and hence can overcome people without fighting. One way that a city can be taken is to attack a place they will be sure to want

ZHANG YU

to save, so as to draw the enemy out of the city stronghold to come to the rescue, and then take the city by sneak attack.

DU MU

When the enemy is in a condition that you can take advantage of, if you do not lose the opportunity to crush them as if they were dry rot, then it will not take long.

MASTER SUN

IT IS IMPERATIVE TO CONTEST ALL FACTIONS FOR COMPLETE VICTORY, SO THE ARMY IS NOT GARRISONED AND THE PROFIT CAN BE TOTAL. THIS IS THE LAW OF STRATEGIC SIEGE.

CAO CAO

You do not fight with your enemy, but you do win completely, establishing victory everywhere, not garrisoning armies and bloodying blades.

MEI YAOCHEN

Complete victory is when the army does not fight, the city is not besieged, the destruction does not go on long, but in each case the enemy is overcome by strategy. This is called strategic siege. In this way you do not dull your army, and your profit is naturally complete.

ZHANG YU

If you do not fight, your soldiers will not be wounded, if you do not lay siege, your strength will not be exhausted, if you do not continue long, your resources will not be used up. This is how you establish yourself completely victorious over the world. Thereby there are none of the ills associated with garrisons and violence, and there are the benefits of a prosperous country and a strong army. This is the good general's art of strategic siege.

MASTER SUN

SO THE RULE FOR USE OF THE MILITARY IS THAT IF YOU OUTNUMBER THE OPPONENT TEN TO ONE, THEN SURROUND THEM; FIVE TO ONE, ATTACK; TWO TO ONE, DIVIDE.

CAO CAO

When you outnumber the enemy ten to one, then surround them—that is, if the generals are equal in intelligence and bravery, and the soldiers are equal in competence. When you outnumber the enemy five to one, use three fifths of your forces for direct attacks, the other two fifths for surprise attacks. If you outnumber the enemy two to one, then divide your forces into two parts, one for direct assault and one for surprise attacks.

It takes ten times as many soldiers to surround an opponent, because you have to set your encirclement up at some distance from the enemy, so the area you are covering is large, and you have to be on strict guard, thus if you do not have a lot of soldiers there will be gaps and leaks.

      Now if there is division among the ranks of the enemy, so that there is no coherent chain of command, then they will fall apart by themselves, even if you do not surround them. If you do surround them under such circumstances, needless to say they will be annihilated. When Master Sun says you need ten times their number to surround the enemy, this is when your leaders are equal in intelligence and courage and your soldiers are equal in competence, not when there is dissension in the enemy's own ranks.

DU MU

When you calculate and compare the strength of your forces and those of your opponent, take into account the talent, intelligence, and courage of the generals—if you are ten times stronger than the enemy, this is ten to one, and you can surround them, foiling any attempts to get away.

HO YANXI

If you are five to one against your opponent, then you should take three fifths of your forces, divide them into three units to attack the enemy from one side, keeping back two fifths, watching for points of unpreparedness on the opponent's part, and taking advantage of them by surprise attacks.

DU MU

When your forces are said to be five times those of the enemy, this just means you have extra power. Their forces are deployed here and there, so how could you attack them by only three routes? The specific numbers here only refer to attacking a citadel.

CHEN HAO

If you are two to one against your opponent, you should take part of your forces and have them head for the opponent's critical points, or attack some point that the opponent will surely go to defend, so that the

DU MU

opponent will split off to go to the rescue, and you can use the other part of your forces to strike them. The principles of war are not a matter of numbers—in every engagement there are both surprise and frontal attacks, and you do not wait until you have a lot of soldiers to set up reserves for surprise attacks.

DU YOU

When you outnumber the opponent two to one, then one part of your attack force makes a direct assault, one part makes surprise strikes. As they are insufficient to adapt, this confuses the opponent's soldiers and separates them from their army. So a great warrior-emperor said, "If you cannot divide and move, you cannot talk about surprise maneuvers."

MASTER SUN

IF YOU ARE EQUAL, THEN FIGHT IF YOU ARE ABLE. IF YOU ARE FEWER, THEN KEEP AWAY IF YOU ARE ABLE. IF YOU ARE NOT AS GOOD, THEN FLEE IF YOU ARE ABLE.

CAO CAO

If your forces are equal to those of the enemy, even if you are good you should still set up ambushes and surprise attacks to prevail over them. Otherwise, be defensive and do not engage in battle, or if outmatched, take your soldiers and run away.

WANG XI

To be able means to be able to motivate others to fight to the death. If you seize victory by raids and ambushes, this is called superiority in intelligence. It is not a matter of clash of armies.

LI QUAN

If you calculate your power to be less than that of the opponent, then strengthen your defense, do not go out and get your edge snapped. Wait until the mood of the enemy gets sluggish, and then go out and attack by surprise.

DU MU

If your forces are not equal to those of the enemy, avoid their edge for the time being, waiting for a gap; then make a determined bid for victory. To be able also means to be able to endure anger and humiliation, not going out to meet the opponent's challenges.

CHEN HAO

That is not so. It just means that if the enemy's soldiers are more than

yours, then you should run away from them, thereby making them haughty and using this in your future plans. It does not mean enduring anger and humiliation.

JIA LIN

If they are more numerous than you, retreat and hide your troop formations so that the enemy does not know, then set out ambushers to lie in wait for them, set up ruses to confuse them. This, too, is a way of victory.

ZHANG YU

The advice to keep away and not do battle if the opponent is more numerous also applies to the case where all else is equal, the quality of the leadership and of the troops. If your forces are orderly while theirs are chaotic, if you are excited and they are sluggish, then even if they are more numerous you can do battle. If your soldiers, strength, strategy, and courage are all less than that of the opponent, then you should retreat and watch for an opening.

MASTER SUN

THEREFORE IF THE SMALLER SIDE IS STUBBORN, IT BECOMES THE CAPTIVE OF THE LARGER SIDE.

LI QUAN

If the smaller side battles stubbornly without taking its strength into account, it will surely be captured by the larger side.

MENG SHI

The small cannot stand up to the large—this means that if a small country does not assess its power and dares to become the enemy of a large country, no matter how firm its defenses be, it will inevitably become a captive nation. The *Spring and Autumn Annals* say, "If you cannot be strong, and yet cannot be weak, this will result in your defeat."

HO YANXI

Ho Yanxi told the story of Right General Su Jian of the Han dynasty, a vice-general in the wars with the invading Huns of ancient times. Right General Su and Forward General Zhao of the Forward Army were leading a division of several thousand troops when he encountered a Hunnish force ten times as large.

They fought all day, until the Chinese army was decimated. Now Forward General Zhao, a foreigner who had earlier surrendered to the

Chinese in exchange for rank and title, was invited by the Huns to join them, so he took the rest of his mounted troops, about eight hundred or so, and surrendered to the Shanyu, the Hunnish chieftain. Right General Su, now having lost his entire army, was at a loss to know where to go, being the sole survivor.

The great general asked several of his top advisers what to do about the case of Right General Su. One said, "We have not executed a single vice-general on this campaign. Now this Su Jian has deserted his army—we should execute him to show how serious we are."

But another said, "No, that is not right. The rule of martial arts says that it is the very stubbornness of the smaller side that makes it the captive of the larger side. Now this Su was alone with a few thousand troops when he ran into the Shanyu with a few tens of thousands; he fought hard for over a day, not daring to have any other thought as long as any of his soldiers were left. If we execute him now that he has come back by himself, this would be showing people there is no sense in returning!"

GENERALS ARE ASSISTANTS OF THE NATION. WHEN THEIR ASSISTANCE IS COMPLETE, THE COUNTRY IS STRONG. WHEN THEIR ASSISTANCE IS DEFECTIVE, THE COUNTRY IS WEAK.   MASTER SUN

When the generals are completely thorough, their plans do not leak out. If they are defective, their formations are revealed outside.   CAO CAO

The strength or weakness of a country depends on its generals. If the generals help the leadership and are thoroughly capable, then the country will be strong. If the generals do not help the leadership, and harbor duplicity in their hearts, then the country will be weak. Therefore it is imperative to be careful in choosing people for positions of responsibility.   JIA LIN

Complete means having both ability and intelligence. When a country has generals that are thoroughly able and intelligent, then that country is safe and strong. This means that generals have to be completely capable and completely knowledgeable in all operations. Generals in the   HO YANXI field must already be acquainted with all the sciences of warfare before they can command their own soldiers and assess battle formations.

WANG XI

Complete means that when generals are good and wise, then they are both loyal and capable. To be lacking means to be missing something.

ZHANG YU

When the strategy of the generals is thoroughgoing, opponents cannot see into it, so the country is strong. If there is even a slight gap, then opponents can take aggressive advantage of this, so the country is weak.

MASTER SUN

SO THERE ARE THREE WAYS IN WHICH A CIVIL LEADERSHIP CAUSES THE MILITARY TROUBLE. WHEN A CIVIL LEADERSHIP UNAWARE OF THE FACTS TELLS ITS ARMIES TO ADVANCE WHEN IT SHOULD NOT, OR TELLS ITS ARMIES TO RETREAT WHEN IT SHOULD NOT, THIS IS CALLED TYING UP THE ARMIES. WHEN THE CIVIL LEADERSHIP IS IGNORANT OF MILITARY AFFAIRS BUT SHARES EQUALLY IN THE GOVERNMENT OF THE ARMIES, THE SOLDIERS GET CONFUSED. WHEN THE CIVIL LEADERSHIP IS IGNORANT OF MILITARY MANEUVERS BUT SHARES EQUALLY IN THE COMMAND OF THE ARMIES, THE SOLDIERS HESITATE. ONCE THE ARMIES ARE CONFUSED AND HESITANT, TROUBLE COMES FROM COMPETITORS. THIS IS CALLED TAKING AWAY VICTORY BY DERANGING THE MILITARY.

WANG XI

To get rid of these problems, it is necessary to delegate unbridled authority, so it is imperative that officers who are to be generals be both loyal and talented.

DU MU

If the military were to be governed in the same way as ordinary civilian society, then the soldiers would be confused, because there are already customs of military procedure and command in effect.

MEI YAOCHEN

Military and civil affairs are different, dealing with different matters. If you try to use the methods of civilian government to govern a military operation, the operation will become confused.

ZHANG YU

A nation can be governed by humanity and justice, but not an army. An

HORSE AND RIDER
Western Han period, 206 B.C.E–8 C.E.

army can be guided by maneuvering, but not a nation. When there are among civilian officials attached to military commands those who do not know about military strategy, if they are allowed to share in the responsibilities of the military leadership, then the chain of command will not be unified, and the soldiers will become hesitant.

DU MU

Also, if a general lacks the planning ability to assess the officers and place them in positions where they can use the best of their abilities, instead assigning them automatically and thus not making full use of their talents, then the army will become hesitant.

Huang Shigong said, "Those who are good at delegating responsibility employ the intelligent, the brave, the greedy, and the foolish. The intelligent are glad to establish their merit, the brave like to act out their ambitions, the greedy welcome an opportunity to pursue profit, and the foolish do not care if they die."

If your own army is hesitant and confused, you bring trouble on yourself, as if you were to bring enemies in to overcome you.

MENG SHI

When the army troops are in doubt about their responsibilities and confused about what to do, then competitors will take advantage of this disorganized condition and cause trouble.

MASTER SUN

SO THERE ARE FIVE WAYS OF KNOWING WHO WILL WIN. THOSE WHO KNOW WHEN TO FIGHT AND WHEN NOT TO FIGHT ARE VICTORIOUS. THOSE WHO DISCERN WHEN TO USE MANY OR FEW TROOPS ARE VICTORIOUS. THOSE WHOSE UPPER AND LOWER RANKS HAVE THE SAME DESIRE ARE VICTORIOUS. THOSE WHO FACE THE UNPREPARED WITH PREPARATION ARE VICTORIOUS. THOSE WHOSE GENERALS ARE ABLE AND ARE NOT CONSTRAINED BY THEIR GOVERNMENTS ARE VICTORIOUS. THESE FIVE ARE THE WAYS TO KNOW WHO WILL WIN.

HO YANXI

Assess yourselves and your opponents.

DU YOU

Sometimes a large group cannot effectively attack a small group, and then again sometimes weakness can be used to control the strong. Those who can adapt to the situation are victorious. This is why tradition in

the *Spring and Autumn Annals* says, "Military conquest is a matter of coordination, not of masses."

ZHANG YU

Among the methods of deploying troops, there are ways by which a few can overcome many, and there are ways in which many can overcome a few. It is a matter of assessing their use and not misapplying them.

Also, when the generals are all of one mind, the armies coordinate their efforts, and everyone wants to fight, then no one can stand up to such a force.

Be invincible at all times, so as to be prepared for opponents. As Wu Qi said, "When you go out the door, be as if you were seeing an enemy." And Shi Li said, "Be prepared, and you will not be defeated."

When generals have intelligence and courage, they should be entrusted with the responsibility to accomplish their work, and not controlled by civilians.

JIA LIN

The movements of the armies must adapt to the situation on the spot—nothing causes more trouble than trying to run them from behind the lines.

WANG XI

If the civilian leadership tries to control able generals, it will be unable to eliminate hesitation and avoidance. An enlightened leadership is one that knows its people and can delegate authority effectively. In the field it is necessary to take advantage of opportunities as they present themselves, without hesitation—how can this be controlled from far away?

HO YANXI

As a rule, in a military operation you need to change tactics a hundred times at every pace, proceeding when you see you can, falling back when you know there is an impasse. To talk about government orders for all this is like going to announce to your superiors that you want to put out a fire—by the time you get back with an order, there is nothing left but ashes.

DU MU

Du Mu quoted Wei Liaozi, saying, "The general is not controlled by heaven above, is not controlled by earth below, is not controlled by humanity in between. This is why 'the military is an instrument of ill omen.' The general is an officer of death."

SO IT IS SAID THAT IF YOU KNOW OTHERS AND KNOW YOURSELF, YOU WILL NOT BE IMPERILED IN A HUNDRED BATTLES; IF YOU DO NOT KNOW OTHERS BUT KNOW YOURSELF, YOU WIN ONE AND LOSE ONE; IF YOU DO NOT KNOW OTHERS AND DO NOT KNOW YOURSELF, YOU WILL BE IMPERILED IN EVERY SINGLE BATTLE.

MASTER SUN

If you assess your strength and can fend off opponents, what danger is there? If because of your own strength you fail to measure opponents, then victory is uncertain.

LI QUAN

Compare your government to that of the enemy; compare your military leadership to that of the enemy; compare your logistics to that of your enemy; compare your ground to that of your enemy. Having established these comparisons, you will have a preview of superiorities and inferiorities, weaknesses and strengths; this will enable you to prevail every time in subsequent military operations.

DU MU

When you know others, then you are able to attack them. When you know yourself, you are able to protect yourself. Attack is the time for defense, defense is a strategy of attack. If you know this, you will not be in danger even if you fight a hundred battles.

ZHANG YU

When you only know yourself, this means guarding your energy and waiting. This is why knowing defense but not offense means half victory and half defeat.

When you know neither the arts of defense nor the arts of attack, you will lose in battle.

NINE DRAGONS (detail) 1244, by Chen Rong
Francis Gardner Curtis Fund. Courtesy of the Museum of Fine Arts, Boston

FORMATION

You see the inner conditions of opponents by means of their external formations. The inner condition of the formless is inscrutable, whereas that of those who have adopted a specific form is obvious. The inscrutable win, the obvious lose.

DU MU

Those skilled in military operations are able to change their formations in such a way as to ensure victory based on the actions of opponents.

WANG XI

This means the offensive and defensive formations used by two armies. When they are hidden within, they cannot be known to others; when they are visible without, opponents can come in through the chinks. Formation is revealed by attack and defense, so discussion of formation follows the discussion of planning a siege.

ZHANG YU

IN ANCIENT TIMES SKILLFUL WARRIORS FIRST MADE THEMSELVES IN-VINCIBLE, AND THEN WATCHED FOR VULNERABILITY IN THEIR OPPO-NENTS.

MASTER SUN

Making yourself invincible means knowing yourself; waiting for vulner-ability in opponents means knowing others.

ZHANG YU

Hide your form, be orderly within, and watch for gaps and slack.

MEI YAOCHEN

INVINCIBILITY IS IN ONESELF, VULNERABILITY IS IN THE OPPONENT.   MASTER SUN

Keeping your own military in order, always being prepared for opposi-   DU MU
tion, erase your tracks and hide your form, making yourself inscrutable
to opponents. When you see that an opponent can be taken advantage
of, then you emerge to attack.

Invincibility is a matter of self-defense; vulnerability is simply a matter   WANG XI
of having gaps.

THEREFORE SKILLFUL WARRIORS ARE ABLE TO BE INVINCIBLE, BUT   MASTER SUN
THEY CANNOT CAUSE OPPONENTS TO BE VULNERABLE.

If opponents have no formation to find out, no gap or slack to take ad-   DU MU
vantage of, how can you overcome them even if you are well equipped?

If you hide your form, conceal your tracks, and always remain strictly   ZHANG YU
prepared, then you can be invulnerable yourself. If the forms of strength
and weakness of opponents are not outwardly manifest, then how can
you be assured of victory over them?

THAT IS WHY IT IS SAID THAT VICTORY CAN BE DISCERNED BUT NOT   MASTER SUN
MANUFACTURED.

Victory can be discerned to the extent that you see a set formation; but   CAO CAO
to the extent that the enemy has preparations, it cannot be manufactured.

You can only know if your own strength is sufficient to overcome an op-   DU MU
ponent; you cannot force the opponent to slack off to your advantage.

When you have assessed the opponent and seen the opponent's forma-   DU YOU
tion, then you can tell who will win. If the opponent is inscrutable and
formless, then you cannot presume victory.

The victory that can be known is up to you, meaning that you are pre-   HO YANXI pared. The victory that cannot be manufactured is up to the opponent, meaning that the opponent has no form.

MASTER SUN   INVINCIBILITY IS A MATTER OF DEFENSE, VULNERABILITY IS A MATTER OF ATTACK.

CAO CAO   For an invincible defense, conceal your form. When opponents attack you, then they are vulnerable.

DU MU   As long as you have not seen vulnerable formations in opponents, you hide your own form, preparing yourself in such a way as to be invincible, in order to preserve yourself. When opponents have vulnerable formations, then it is time to go out to attack them.

ZHANG YU   When you know you do not yet have the means to conquer, you guard your energy and wait. When you know that an opponent is vulnerable, then you attack the heart and take it.

WANG XI   Those on the defensive are so because they do not have enough to win; those on the offense are so because they have more than enough to win.

MASTER SUN   DEFENSE IS FOR TIMES OF INSUFFICIENCY, ATTACK IS FOR TIMES OF SURPLUS.

LI QUAN   Those whose strength is insufficient should defend, those whose strength is superabundant can attack.

ZHANG YU   When we are on the defensive, it is because there is some lack in terms of a way to seize victory. So we wait for what we need. When we are on the offensive, it is because we already have more than enough of what it takes to overcome an opponent. So we go forth and strike. This means that we will not do battle unless we are certain of complete victory, we will not fight unless we are sure it is safe. Some people think insufficiency means weakness and surplus means strength, but this impression is wrong.

THOSE SKILLED IN DEFENSE HIDE IN THE DEEPEST DEPTHS OF THE EARTH, THOSE SKILLED IN ATTACK MANEUVER IN THE HIGHEST HEIGHTS OF THE SKY. THEREFORE THEY CAN PRESERVE THEMSELVES AND ACHIEVE COMPLETE VICTORY.

MASTER SUN

They hide in the depths of the earth by taking advantage of the fastness of the mountains, rivers, and hills. They maneuver in the heights of the sky by taking advantage of the times of nature.

CAO CAO

In defense, you hush your voices and obliterate your tracks, hidden as ghosts and spirits beneath the earth, invisible to anyone. On the attack, your movement is swift and your cry shattering, fast as thunder and lightning, as though coming from the sky, impossible to prepare for.

DU MU

Defense here means lying low when you do not see any effective way to attack, sinking into stillness and recondite silence, not letting opponents find you out. Attack is for when you see an advantage to aim for. On the attack you should be extremely swift, taking advantage of unexpectedness, wary of letting opponents find you out and prepare against you.

WANG XI

TO PERCEIVE VICTORY WHEN IT IS KNOWN TO ALL IS NOT REALLY SKILLFUL. EVERYONE CALLS VICTORY IN BATTLE GOOD, BUT IT IS NOT REALLY GOOD.

MASTER SUN

What everyone knows is what has already happened or become obvious. What the aware individual knows is what has not yet taken shape, what has not yet occurred. Everyone says victory in battle is good, but if you see the subtle and notice the hidden so as to seize victory where there is no form, this is really good.

ZHANG YU

Ordinary people see the means of victory but do not know the forms by which to ensure victory.

WANG XI

Everyone can easily see armed conflict—this takes no skill. Knowledge that does not go beyond what the generality knows is not really good.

LI QUAN

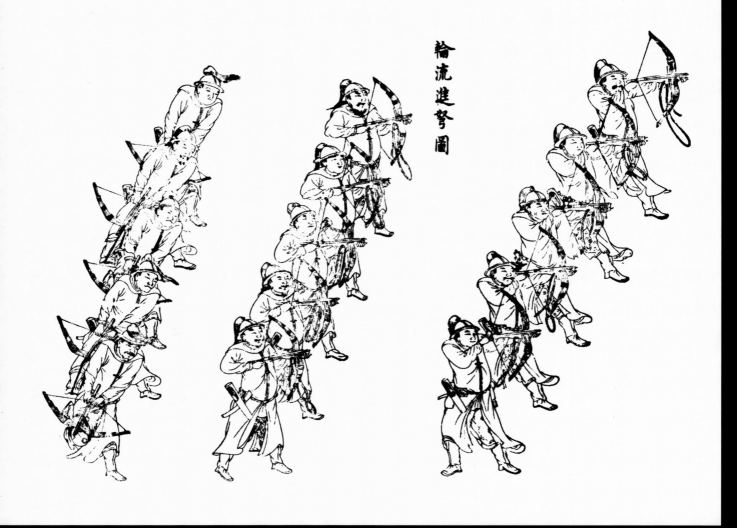

輪流進弩圖

ARCHERS IN FORMATION. Ming dynasty, 1368–1644

Firm in defense, victorious in offense, able to keep whole without ever losing, seeing victory before it happens, accurately recognizing defeat before it occurs—this is called truly subtle penetration of mysteries.

IT DOES NOT TAKE MUCH STRENGTH TO LIFT A HAIR, IT DOES NOT TAKE SHARP EYES TO SEE THE SUN AND MOON, IT DOES NOT TAKE SHARP EARS TO HEAR A THUNDERCLAP.

What everyone knows is not called wisdom, victory over others by forced battle is not considered good.

A military leader of wisdom and ability lays deep plans for what other people do not figure on. This is why Sun Tzu speaks of being unknowable as the dark.

IN ANCIENT TIMES THOSE KNOWN AS GOOD WARRIORS PREVAILED WHEN IT WAS EASY TO PREVAIL.

Find out the subtle points over which it is easy to prevail, attack what can be overcome, do not attack what cannot be overcome.

When the strategy of opponents first makes an appearance, you operate secretly in such a way as to be able to attack it. Since the effort used is little, and your assurance of victory is done in a subtle way, it is said to be easy to prevail.

If you are only able to ensure victory after engaging an opponent in armed conflict, that victory is a hard one. If you see the subtle and notice the hidden, breaking through before formation, that victory is an easy one.

THEREFORE THE VICTORIES OF GOOD WARRIORS ARE NOT NOTED FOR CLEVERNESS OR BRAVERY. THEREFORE THEIR VICTORIES IN BATTLE ARE NOT FLUKES. THEIR VICTORIES ARE NOT FLUKES BECAUSE THEY POSITION THEMSELVES WHERE THEY WILL SURELY WIN, PREVAILING OVER THOSE WHO HAVE ALREADY LOST.

MEI YAOCHEN   Great wisdom is not obvious, great merit is not advertised. When you see the subtle, it is easy to win—what has it to do with bravery or cleverness?

HO YANXI   When trouble is solved before it forms, who calls that clever? When there is victory without battle, who talks about bravery?

ZHANG YU   Secret plotting and covert operations seize victory in formlessness—no one hears of the knowledge that assesses opponents and ensures victory, no one sees the success of those who take the flag and assassinate the generals. The way to be able to win without fail is to see when opponents are in vulnerable formations, and then disposition your forces to prevail over them.

LI QUAN   When the army is old, the soldiers are lazy, and the discipline and command are not unified, this is an opponent that has already lost.

MASTER SUN   SO IT IS THAT GOOD WARRIORS TAKE THEIR STAND ON GROUND WHERE THEY CANNOT LOSE, AND DO NOT OVERLOOK CONDITIONS THAT MAKE AN OPPONENT PRONE TO DEFEAT.

LI QUAN   The army that finds its ground flourishes, the army that loses its ground perishes. Here the ground means a place of strategic importance.

DU MU   Ground where one cannot lose means invincible strategy that makes it impossible for opponents to defeat you. Not overlooking conditions that make opponents prone to defeat means spying out the enemies' vulnerabilities, not missing any of them.

MASTER SUN   THEREFORE A VICTORIOUS ARMY FIRST WINS AND THEN SEEKS BATTLE; A DEFEATED ARMY FIRST BATTLES AND THEN SEEKS VICTORY.

CAO CAO   This is the difference between those with strategy and those without forethought.

HO YANXI   In a military operation, first determine a winning strategy, and only then

GENERAL MINGLIANG. Ch'ing dynasty, 1644-1911

send forth the troops. If you do not plan first, hoping to rely on your strength, your victory is uncertain.

JIA LIN

If you set forth your battle lines and lightly advance without knowing your own condition or that of your opponent, you may be seeking victory, but in the end you defeat yourself.

MASTER SUN

THOSE WHO USE ARMS WELL CULTIVATE THE WAY AND KEEP THE RULES. THUS THEY CAN GOVERN IN SUCH A WAY AS TO PREVAIL OVER THE CORRUPT.

CAO CAO

Skilled users of arms first cultivate the Way that makes them invincible, keep their rules, and do not miss defeatist confusion in opponents.

LI QUAN

Using harmony to hunt down opposition, not attacking a blameless country, not taking captives or booty wherever the army goes, not razing the trees or polluting the wells, washing off and purifying the shrines of the towns and hills in the countryside you pass through, not repeating the mistakes of a moribund nation—all this is called the Way and its rules. When the army is strictly disciplined, to the point where soldiers would die rather than disobey, rewards and punishments that are trustworthy and just are established—when the military leadership is such that it can achieve this, it can prevail over an opponent's corrupt civil government.

MASTER SUN

THE RULES OF THE MILITARY ARE FIVE: MEASUREMENT, ASSESSMENT, CALCULATION, COMPARISON, AND VICTORY. THE GROUND GIVES RISE TO MEASUREMENTS, MEASUREMENTS GIVE RISE TO ASSESSMENTS, ASSESSMENTS GIVE RISE TO CALCULATIONS, CALCULATIONS GIVE RISE TO COMPARISONS, COMPARISONS GIVE RISE TO VICTORIES.

CAO CAO

By the comparison of measurements you know where victory and defeat lie.

WANG XI

The heavy prevail over the light.

THEREFORE A VICTORIOUS ARMY IS LIKE A POUND COMPARED TO A GRAM, A DEFEATED ARMY IS LIKE A GRAM COMPARED TO A POUND.

WHEN THE VICTORIOUS GET THEIR PEOPLE TO GO TO BATTLE AS IF THEY WERE DIRECTING A MASSIVE FLOOD OF WATER INTO A DEEP CANYON, THIS IS A MATTER OF FORMATION.

When water accumulates in a deep canyon, no one can measure its amount, just as our defense shows no form. When the water is released it rushes down in a torrent, just as our attack is irresistible.

FORCE

Force mean s shifts in accumulated energy or momentum. Skillful warriors are able to allow the force of momentum to seize victory for them without exerting their strength.

WANG XI

GOVERNING A LARGE NUMBER AS THOUGH GOVERNING A SMALL NUMBER IS A MATTER OF DIVISION INTO GROUPS. BATTLING A LARGE NUMBER AS THOUGH BATTLING A SMALL NUMBER IS A MATTER OF FORMS AND CALLS.

MASTER SUN

Forms and calls refer to the formations and signals used to dispose troops and coordinate movements.

CAO CAO

MAKING THE ARMIES ABLE TO TAKE ON OPPONENTS WITHOUT BEING DEFEATED IS A MATTER OF UNORTHODOX AND ORTHODOX METHODS.

MASTER SUN

When you meet opponents head on, with coordinated surprise attacks all around, you can always win and never lose.

JIA LIN

A military body goes through myriad transformations, in which everything is blended. Nothing is not orthodox, nothing is not unorthodox. If the militia is raised for a just cause, that is orthodox. If it adapts to change in face of an enemy, that is unorthodox. What is orthodox for you, cause opponents to see as unorthodox; what is unorthodox for you,

HO YANXI

cause opponents to see as orthodox. The orthodox is also unorthodox, and the unorthodox is also orthodox. Generally in military operations there is always the orthodox and the unorthodox, or the straightforward and the surprise—victory without use of both orthodox and unorthodox methods is a lucky win in what amounts to a brawl.

ZHANG YU   Various people have different explanations of what is orthodox and what is unorthodox. Orthodoxy and unorthodoxy are not fixed, but are like a cycle. Emperor Taizong of the Tang dynasty, a famous warrior and administrator, spoke of manipulating opponents' perceptions of what is orthodox and what is unorthodox, then attacking unexpectedly, combining both into one, becoming inscrutable to opponents.

MASTER SUN   FOR THE IMPACT OF ARMED FORCES TO BE LIKE STONES THROWN ON EGGS IS A MATTER OF EMPTINESS AND FULLNESS.

CAO CAO   Attack complete emptiness with complete fullness.

ZHANG YU   A later chapter says that good warriors make others come to them, and do not go to others. This is the principle of emptiness and fullness of others and self. When you induce opponents to come to you, then their force is always empty; as long as you do not go to them, your force is always full. Attacking emptiness with fullness is like throwing stones on eggs—the eggs are sure to break.

MASTER SUN   IN BATTLE, CONFRONTATION IS DONE DIRECTLY, VICTORY IS GAINED BY SURPRISE.

CAO CAO   Direct confrontation is facing opponents head on, surprise forces attack unexpectedly from the sides.

MASTER SUN   THEREFORE THOSE SKILLED AT THE UNORTHODOX ARE INFINITE AS HEAVEN AND EARTH, INEXHAUSTIBLE AS THE GREAT RIVERS. WHEN THEY COME TO AN END, THEY BEGIN AGAIN, LIKE THE DAYS AND MONTHS; THEY DIE AND ARE REBORN, LIKE THE FOUR SEASONS.

LI QUAN	Heaven and earth mean movement and stillness. Rivers represent a ceaseless flux. The changes of unorthodox surprise movements are like the ceaseless changes of the weather cycle.
ZHANG YU	Sun and moon travel through the sky, they set and rise again. The four seasons succeed one another, flourishing and then fading again. This is a metaphor for the interchange of surprise unorthodox movements and orthodox direct confrontation, mixing together into a whole, ending and beginning infinitely.
MASTER SUN	THERE ARE ONLY FIVE NOTES IN THE MUSICAL SCALE, BUT THEIR VARIATIONS ARE SO MANY THAT THEY CANNOT ALL BE HEARD. THERE ARE ONLY FIVE BASIC COLORS, BUT THEIR VARIATIONS ARE SO MANY THAT THEY CANNOT ALL BE SEEN. THERE ARE ONLY FIVE BASIC FLAVORS, BUT THEIR VARIATIONS ARE SO MANY THAT THEY CANNOT ALL BE TASTED. THERE ARE ONLY TWO KINDS OF CHARGE IN BATTLE, THE UNORTHODOX SURPRISE ATTACK AND THE ORTHODOX DIRECT ATTACK, BUT VARIATIONS OF THE UNORTHODOX AND THE ORTHODOX ARE ENDLESS. THE UNORTHODOX AND THE ORTHODOX GIVE RISE TO EACH OTHER, LIKE A BEGINNINGLESS CIRCLE—WHO COULD EXHAUST THEM?
MEI YAOCHEN	The comprehensiveness of adaptive movement is limitless.
WANG XI	Opponents cannot exhaust you.
MASTER SUN	WHEN THE SPEED OF RUSHING WATER REACHES THE POINT WHERE IT CAN MOVE BOULDERS, THIS IS THE FORCE OF MOMENTUM. WHEN THE SPEED OF A HAWK IS SUCH THAT IT CAN STRIKE AND KILL, THIS IS PRECISION. SO IT IS WITH SKILLFUL WARRIORS—THEIR FORCE IS SWIFT, THEIR PRECISION IS CLOSE. THEIR FORCE IS LIKE DRAWING A CATAPULT, THEIR PRECISION IS LIKE RELEASING THE TRIGGER.
DU MU	Their force is swift in the sense that the force of the momentum of battle kills when it is released—that is why it is likened to a drawn catapult.

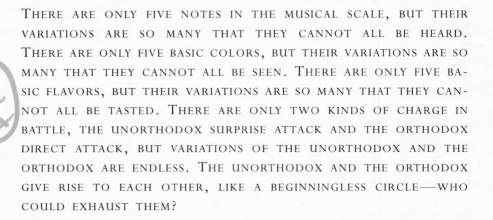

If you presume on the orderliness of government and fail to provide for the comfort of the governed, thus creating much resentment, disorder is certain to arise.

If you presume on order, disorder will arise. If you presume on courage and strength, timidity and weakness will arise.

What this means is that if you want to feign disorder so as to lead opponents on, first you must have complete order, for only then can you create artificial disorder. If you want to feign cowardice to spy on opponents, first you must be extremely brave, for only then can you act artificially timid. If you want to feign weakness to induce haughtiness in opponents, first you must be extremely strong, for only then can you pretend to be weak.

ORDER AND DISORDER ARE A MATTER OF ORGANIZATION, COURAGE AND COWARDICE ARE A MATTER OF MOMENTUM, STRENGTH AND WEAKNESS ARE A MATTER OF FORMATION.

Order and disorder are changes in organization. Organization means methodical regulation. Courage and cowardice are changes in momentum or force. Strength and weakness are changes in formation.

When an army has the force of momentum, even the timid become brave; when it loses the force of momentum, even the brave become timid. Nothing is fixed in the laws of warfare—they develop based on momenta.

The brave act quickly, while the timid drag their feet. When opponents see you are not moving ahead, they will assume you are timid, and will take you lightly. You then take advantage of their laxity to use the force of momentum to attack them.

THEREFORE THOSE WHO SKILLFULLY MOVE OPPONENTS MAKE FORMA-
TIONS THAT OPPONENTS ARE SURE TO FOLLOW, GIVE WHAT OPPO-
NENTS ARE SURE TO TAKE. THEY MOVE OPPONENTS WITH THE
PROSPECT OF GAIN, WAITING FOR THEM IN AMBUSH.

MASTER SUN

Formations that opponents are sure to follow are formations that give
the impression of exhaustion. Opponents are moved by the prospect of
an advantage.

CAO CAO

It does not only mean giving the impression of exhaustion and weakness.
When you are stronger than your opponent, then you appear worn out
to induce the opponent to come to you. When you are weaker than
your opponent, then you appear strong to impel the opponent to go
away. Thus the movements of opponents all follow your direction.
When you move opponents with the prospect of an advantage, since opponents are following you, you wait for them in ambush with well-pre-
pared forces.

DU MU

Whether you get opponents to follow you, or get them to take something, be sure you have crack troops ready for them first.

WANG XI

THEREFORE GOOD WARRIORS SEEK EFFECTIVENESS IN BATTLE FROM
THE FORCE OF MOMENTUM, NOT FROM INDIVIDUAL PEOPLE. THERE-
FORE THEY ARE ABLE TO CHOOSE PEOPLE AND LET THE FORCE OF
MOMENTUM DO ITS WORK.

MASTER SUN

When you have the force of momentum in war, even the timid can be
courageous. So it is possible to choose them for their capabilities and
give them the appropriate responsibilities. The brave can fight, the careful can guard, the intelligent can communicate. No one is useless.

LI QUAN

It is easy to get people to act by means of the force of momentum,
whereas it is hard to demand power in individual people. The able have
to choose the right people and also let the force of momentum do its
work.

MEI YAOCHEN

衛尉安成兵銚期

GUARDSMAN. Ch'ing dynasty, 1644–1911

The rule for delegation of responsibility is to use greed, use folly, use intelligence, and use bravery, allowing for the natural force of each one, not blaming people for what they are incapable of, but choosing appropriate responsibilities for them according to their respective capacities.

GETTING PEOPLE TO FIGHT BY LETTING THE FORCE OF MOMENTUM WORK IS LIKE ROLLING LOGS AND ROCKS. LOGS AND ROCKS ARE STILL WHEN IN A SECURE PLACE, BUT ROLL ON AN INCLINE; THEY REMAIN STATIONARY IF SQUARE, THEY ROLL IF ROUND. THEREFORE, WHEN PEOPLE ARE SKILLFULLY LED INTO BATTLE, THE MOMENTUM IS LIKE THAT OF ROUND ROCKS ROLLING DOWN A HIGH MOUNTAIN—THIS IS FORCE.

Roll rocks down a ten-thousand-foot mountain, and they cannot be stopped—this is because of the mountain, not the rocks. Get people to fight with the courage to win every time, and the strong and the weak unite—this is because of the momentum, not the individuals.

ENSO, by Japanese Zen master Bankei, 1622–93

SIX

EMPTINESS
AND FULLNESS

Militarists avoid the full and strike the empty, so they first have to recognize emptiness and fullness in others and themselves.

DU MU

THOSE WHO ARE FIRST ON THE BATTLEFIELD AND AWAIT THE OPPONENTS ARE AT EASE; THOSE WHO ARE LAST ON THE BATTLEFIELD AND HEAD INTO BATTLE GET WORN OUT.

MASTER SUN

Those who first position themselves in an advantageous place and await opponents there are prepared, so the troops are relaxed. If the opponents are in an advantageous position, then you should not go to them, but withdraw your troops to another base, making it appear that you will not oppose their army. Opponents will then think that you have no strategy, and will come and attack you. Then you can turn things around and make opponents tired without wearing yourself out.

JIA LIN

THEREFORE GOOD WARRIORS CAUSE OTHERS TO COME TO THEM, AND DO NOT GO TO OTHERS.

MASTER SUN

Causing opponents to come to you, you should conserve your strength and wait for them, not going to opponents for fear of wearing yourself out.

DU MU

If you make opponents come to fight, then their force will always be

ZHANG YU

empty. If you do not go to fight, then your force will always be full. This is the art of emptying others and filling yourself.

MASTER SUN WHAT CAUSES OPPONENTS TO COME OF THEIR OWN ACCORD IS THE PROSPECT OF GAIN. WHAT DISCOURAGES OPPONENTS FROM COMING IS THE PROSPECT OF HARM.

HO YANXI Lure them with something to gain, and opponents will be tired while you are at ease.

ZHANG YU The only way to get opponents to come to you is to lure them with gain. The only way to ensure that opponents will not get to you is to harm what they care about.

CAO CAO To bring them to you, lure them with gain. To keep them from getting to you, attack where they will be sure to go to the rescue.

DU YOU If you can cause them to run while you hold an essential pass, you can make it impossible for opponents to get to you. As it is said, "One cat at the hole, and ten thousand mice dare not come out; one tiger in the valley, and ten thousand deer cannot pass through."

MASTER SUN SO WHEN OPPONENTS ARE AT EASE, IT IS POSSIBLE TO TIRE THEM. WHEN THEY ARE WELL FED, IT IS POSSIBLE TO STARVE THEM. WHEN THEY ARE AT REST, IT IS POSSIBLE TO MOVE THEM.

CAO CAO You cause them trouble with some affair, you cut off their supply routes to starve them, you attack what they like and appear where they will go, thus causing opponents to have to go to the rescue.

LI QUAN You attack unexpectedly, causing opponents to become exhausted just running for their lives. You burn their supplies and raze their fields, cutting off their supply routes. You appear at critical places and strike when they least expect it, making them have to go to the rescue.

DU MU The arts of starving an opponent do not stop at cutting off supply lines.

LOKAPALA
"heavenly king"
Tang dynasty, 618-906

In the late sixth century, Yuwen Huaji led an armed force to attack Li Mi. Li Mi knew that Huaji was short on supplies, so he feigned conciliation in order to wear out his troops. Huaji was delighted, and fed his soldiers all they wanted, expecting that Li Mi was going to supply them. Subsequently the food ran out, and the generals from Li Mi's army who had pretended to join up with Huaji went back to Li Mi's camp with their troops. This finally led to Huaji's defeat.

MASTER SUN

APPEAR WHERE THEY CANNOT GO, HEAD FOR WHERE THEY LEAST EXPECT YOU. TO TRAVEL HUNDREDS OF MILES WITHOUT FATIGUE, GO OVER LAND WHERE THERE ARE NO PEOPLE.

CAO CAO

Make it impossible for the enemy to get there to the rescue. Appear where there is an opening and strike at a gap; avoid where they are guarding, hit where they are not expecting it.

CHEN HAO

Striking at an open gap does not only mean where the opponent has no defense. As long as the defense is not strict, the place is not tightly guarded, the generals are weak and the troops are disorderly, the supplies are scarce and the forces are isolated, if you face them with an orderly and prepared army, they will fall apart in front of you. This way you do not need to labor and suffer, for it is as if you were traveling over unpopulated territory.

MASTER SUN

TO UNFAILINGLY TAKE WHAT YOU ATTACK, ATTACK WHERE THERE IS NO DEFENSE. FOR UNFAILINGLY SECURE DEFENSE, DEFEND WHERE THERE IS NO ATTACK.

DU MU

If they are alert on their eastern flank, strike on their western flank. Lure them on from the front, strike them from behind.

LI QUAN

It is easy to take over from those who have not thought ahead.

CHEN HAO

Do not figure on opponents not attacking; worry about your own lack of preparation. When you can attack anywhere and defend everywhere, your military strategy is complete.

Attack their gaps: incompetence on the part of the military leadership, lack of training among the troops, insubstantiality in fortifications, lack of strictness in preparations, inability to effect rescues, shortages of food, psychological disunity. Defend with fullness: competence in the military leaders, excellence in the soldiers, solidity in fortifications, strictness in preparation, ability to effect rescues, sufficiency of food, psychological unity.

WANG XI

Those who are good on the attack maneuver in the heights of the skies, making it impossible for opponents to prepare for them. If no one can prepare for you, then where you attack is unguarded. Those who are good on the defense hide in the depths of the earth, making it impossible for opponents to fathom them. If you are unfathomable, then what you guard is not attacked by opponents.

ZHANG YU

SO IN THE CASE OF THOSE WHO ARE SKILLED IN ATTACK, THEIR OPPONENTS DO NOT KNOW WHERE TO DEFEND. IN THE CASE OF THOSE SKILLED IN DEFENSE, THEIR OPPONENTS DO NOT KNOW WHERE TO ATTACK.

MASTER SUN

This means true information is not leaked.

CAO CAO

When directives are carried out, people are sincerely loyal, preparations for defense are firmly secured, and yet you are so subtle and secretive that you reveal no form, opponents are unsure—their intelligence is of no avail.

JIA LIN

Those good at attack do not divulge their operational secrets; those good at defense prepare thoroughly, without gaps.

MEI YAOCHEN

BE EXTREMELY SUBTLE, EVEN TO THE POINT OF FORMLESSNESS. BE EXTREMELY MYSTERIOUS, EVEN TO THE POINT OF SOUNDLESSNESS. THEREBY YOU CAN BE THE DIRECTOR OF THE OPPONENT'S FATE.

MASTER SUN

The subtle is stillness, the mysterious is movement. Stillness is defense, movement is attack. Whether opponents live or die depends on you, so you are as though director of their fate.

DU MU

SCENE OF SKIRMISH. Western Wei dynasty, 535–56 C.E.

This means being so subtle as to be imperceptible, and to be able to change suddenly like a mysterious spirit.

DU YOU

Formlessness means being so subtle and secret that no one can spy on you. Soundlessness means being so mysteriously swift that no one notices you.

MEI YAOCHEN

TO ADVANCE IRRESISTIBLY, PUSH THROUGH THEIR GAPS. TO RETREAT ELUSIVELY, OUTSPEED THEM.

MASTER SUN

If your forces push through the opponent's gaps as they move forward and take advantage of speed when they retreat, then you can overcome the opponent while the opponent cannot overcome you.

HO YANXI

At a standoff, if you rush in and strike when you see a gap, how can the enemy fend you off? Having gained the advantage, you retreat, hastening back to your stronghold for self-defense—then how can the enemy pursue you? Military conditions are based on speed—come like the wind, go like lightning, and opponents will be unable to overcome you.

ZHANG YU

THEREFORE WHEN YOU WANT TO DO BATTLE, EVEN IF THE OPPONENT IS DEEPLY ENTRENCHED IN A DEFENSIVE POSITION, HE WILL BE UNABLE TO AVOID FIGHTING IF YOU ATTACK WHERE HE WILL SURELY GO TO THE RESCUE.

MASTER SUN

Cut off their supply routes, guard their return routes, and attack their civilian leadership.

CAO CAO AND LI QUAN

If you are on your home territory and the opponents are invaders, then cut off their supplies and guard their return routes. If you are on the opponent's home ground, then attack the civilian leadership.

DU MU

WHEN YOU DO NOT WANT TO DO BATTLE, EVEN IF YOU DRAW A LINE ON THE GROUND TO HOLD, THE OPPONENT CANNOT FIGHT WITH YOU BECAUSE YOU SET HIM OFF ON THE WRONG TRACK.

MASTER SUN

LI QUAN   Set opponents off on the wrong track by baffling them so that they cannot fight with you.

DU MU   This means that when opponents come to attack you, you do not fight with them but rather set up a strategic change to confuse them and make them uncertain, deflecting them from their original intention to attack, making them reluctant to fight with you.

ZHANG YU   When you are on your home ground and are well supplied compared to the number of soldiers you have, while opponents are on alien territory and have little food compared to their number, then it is to your advantage not to fight. If you want to be sure opponents will not dare come to do battle with you even though you are not heavily fortified, let them see a setup that confuses them and deflects their course. For example, when Sima Yi was going to attack Zhuge Liang, Zhuge took down his flags and put away his battle drums, opened the gates and swept the road. Yi suspected an ambush, so he withdrew his forces and fled.

MASTER SUN   THEREFORE WHEN YOU INDUCE OTHERS TO CONSTRUCT A FORMATION WHILE YOU YOURSELF ARE FORMLESS, THEN YOU ARE CONCENTRATED WHILE THE OPPONENT IS DIVIDED.

ZHANG YU   What is orthodox to you, make opponents see as unorthodox; what is unorthodox to you, make them see as orthodox. This is inducing others to construct a formation. To be able to use the unorthodox as orthodox and use the orthodox as unorthodox, changing in a whirl, making yourself unfathomable to opponents, is being formless. Once the opponent's formation is seen, you then mass your troops against it. Since your form is not revealed, the opponent will surely divide up his forces for security.

MASTER SUN   WHEN YOU ARE CONCENTRATED INTO ONE WHILE THE OPPONENT IS DIVIDED INTO TEN, YOU ARE ATTACKING AT A CONCENTRATION OF TEN TO ONE, SO YOU OUTNUMBER THE OPPONENT.

ZHANG YU   Seeing where the enemy is solid and where the enemy is insubstantial, you do not go to the trouble of elaborate preparations and therefore are concentrated into one garrison. The enemy, on the other hand, not seeing your form, therefore divides up to cover numerous points—so you with your whole force strike individual fragments of the enemy. Thus you inevitably outnumber them.

IF YOU CAN STRIKE FEW WITH MANY, YOU WILL THUS MINIMIZE THE NUMBER OF THOSE WITH WHOM YOU DO BATTLE.

MASTER SUN

While being deeply entrenched and highly barricaded, not allowing any information about yourself to become known, go out and in formlessly, attacking and taking unfathomably. Harry and confuse enemies so that they divide their troops in fear, trying to cover themselves on all sides. It is like climbing a high mountain to spy on a citadel—seeing out from behind a veil, you know all about the disposition of the enemy personnel, while the enemy cannot figure out your offense or defense. Therefore you can be unified while the enemy is divided. The power of those who are united is whole, while the power of those who are divided is reduced. By striking diminished power with whole power, it is possible always to win.

DU MU

YOUR BATTLEGROUND IS NOT TO BE KNOWN, FOR WHEN IT CANNOT BE KNOWN, THE ENEMY MAKES MANY GUARD OUTPOSTS, AND SINCE MULTIPLE OUTPOSTS ARE ESTABLISHED, YOU ONLY HAVE TO DO BATTLE WITH SMALL SQUADS.

MASTER SUN

When your form is concealed, the enemy is in doubt, and so divides up his company to be on guard against you. This means that enemy groups are small and easy to hit.

CAO CAO

Don't let the enemy know where you will clash, for if they know they will mass their strength to resist you.

WANG XI

SO WHEN THE FRONT IS PREPARED, THE REAR IS LACKING, AND WHEN THE REAR IS PREPARED THE FRONT IS LACKING. PREPAREDNESS ON THE LEFT MEANS LACK ON THE RIGHT, PREPAREDNESS ON THE RIGHT

MASTER SUN

MEANS LACK ON THE LEFT. PREPAREDNESS EVERYWHERE MEANS LACK EVERYWHERE.

DU YOU

This means that when troops are on guard in many places, they are perforce scattered into small bands.

MASTER SUN

THE FEW ARE THOSE ON THE DEFENSIVE AGAINST OTHERS, THE MANY ARE THOSE WHO CAUSE OTHERS TO BE ON THE DEFENSIVE AGAINST THEMSELVES.

MEI YAOCHEN

The more defenses you induce your enemy to adopt, the more impoverished your enemy will be.

MASTER SUN

SO IF YOU KNOW THE PLACE AND TIME OF BATTLE, YOU CAN JOIN THE FIGHT FROM A THOUSAND MILES AWAY. IF YOU DO NOT KNOW THE PLACE AND TIME OF BATTLE, THEN YOUR LEFT FLANK CANNOT SAVE YOUR RIGHT, YOUR RIGHT CANNOT SAVE YOUR LEFT, YOUR VANGUARD CANNOT SAVE YOUR REARGUARD, AND YOUR REARGUARD CANNOT SAVE YOUR VANGUARD, EVEN IN A SHORT RANGE OF A FEW TO A FEW DOZEN MILES.

DU YOU

The ancient philosopher Master Guan said, "Go forth armed without determining strategy, and you will destroy yourself in battle."

MASTER SUN

ACCORDING TO MY ASSESSMENT, EVEN IF YOU HAVE MANY MORE TROOPS THAN OTHERS, HOW CAN THAT HELP YOU TO VICTORY?

LI QUAN

If you do not know the place and time of battle, even though your troops outnumber others, how can you know whether you will win or lose?

MASTER SUN

SO IT IS SAID THAT VICTORY CAN BE MADE.

MENG SHI

If you cause opponents to be unaware of the place and time of battle, you can always win.

MASTER SUN

EVEN IF OPPONENTS ARE NUMEROUS, THEY CAN BE MADE NOT TO FIGHT.

GUAN DI, circa 1550-1640
Courtesy of the Victoria and Albert
Picture Library, London

JIA LIN	Even though opponents be numerous, if they do not know the conditions of your troops and you constantly make them rush about trying to cover themselves, they will not have time to formulate battle plans.
ZHANG YU	Divide their forces, do not let them press forward at once with coordinated strength—then how could anyone fight with you?
MASTER SUN	SO ASSESS THEM TO FIND OUT THEIR PLANS, BOTH THE SUCCESSFUL ONES AND THE FAILURES. INCITE THEM TO ACTION IN ORDER TO FIND OUT THE PATTERNS OF THEIR MOVEMENT AND REST.
MENG SHI	Assess opponents' conditions, observe what they do, and you can find out their plans and measures.
CHEN HAO	Do something for or against them, making opponents turn their attention to it, so that you can find out their patterns of aggressive and defensive behavior.
DU MU	Stir opponents up, making them respond to you; then you can observe their forms of behavior, and whether they are orderly or confused. The military wizard Wu Qi devised this strategy for assessing generals: have brave young men lead crack troops on strikes and run away after skirmishing, without being punished for running away. Then observe the enemy's behavior—if there is orderly rule, and the enemy does not give chase to the fleeing troops and does not try to take advantage to grab what it can, this means the general has a strategy. On the other hand, if the enemy behaves like a mob, giving chase in total confusion and greedily trying to plunder, you can be sure that the directives of the generals are not carried out, so you can attack them without hesitation.
MASTER SUN	INDUCE THEM TO ADOPT SPECIFIC FORMATIONS, IN ORDER TO KNOW THE GROUND OF DEATH AND LIFE.
LI QUAN	When you break ranks and set up guerrilla squads, you may lay down your banners and drums, your signals and symbols of military organization, to use the appearance of weakness in order to induce them to adopt a specific form. Or you may set up false arrays of campfires and

banners, to use the appearance of strength in order to induce them to adopt a specific form. If you die by going to them and live by getting them to come to you, this way death and life come about depending on the ground.

The ground of death and life is the battleground. If you go to the enemy on a ground of death you will live, while if you leave the enemy on a ground of life you will die. This means that you use many methods to confuse and disturb enemies to observe the forms of their response to you; after that you deal with them accordingly, so you can know what sort of situations mean life and what sort of situations mean death.

DU MU

TEST THEM TO FIND OUT WHERE THEY ARE SUFFICIENT AND WHERE THEY ARE LACKING.

MASTER SUN

Compare where you are sufficient with where the enemy is sufficient, compare where you are lacking with where the enemy is lacking.

DU MU

Compare the strength of the enemy with your own, and you will know where there is sufficiency or lack. After that you can assess the advantages of attack or defense.

WANG XI

THEREFORE THE CONSUMMATION OF FORMING AN ARMY IS TO ARRIVE AT FORMLESSNESS. WHEN YOU HAVE NO FORM, UNDERCOVER ESPIONAGE CANNOT FIND OUT ANYTHING, INTELLIGENCE CANNOT FORM A STRATEGY.

MASTER SUN

First you use emptiness and fullness to induce the enemy to adopt a specific formation while remaining unfathomable to the enemy, so that ultimately you reach formlessness. Once you have no perceptible form, you leave no traces to follow, so spies cannot find any chinks to see through and those in charge of intelligence cannot put any plans into operation.

ZHANG YU

VICTORY OVER MULTITUDES BY MEANS OF FORMATION IS UNKNOWABLE TO THE MULTITUDES. EVERYONE KNOWS THE FORM BY WHICH I AM VICTORIOUS, BUT NO ONE KNOWS THE FORM BY WHICH I ENSURE VICTORY.

MASTER SUN

The multitudes know when you win, but they do not know that it is based on the formations of the enemy. They know the traces of attainment of victory, but do not know the abstract form that makes for victory.

MEI YAOCHEN

Victory in war is apparent to all, but the science of ensuring victory is a mysterious secret, generally unknown.

LI QUAN

THEREFORE VICTORY IN WAR IS NOT REPETITIOUS, BUT ADAPTS ITS FORM ENDLESSLY.

MASTER SUN

Determining changes as appropriate, do not repeat former strategies to gain victory.

LI QUAN

Whatever formations opponents may adopt, from the beginning I can adapt to them to attain victory.

DU MU

MILITARY FORMATION IS LIKE WATER—THE FORM OF WATER IS TO AVOID THE HIGH AND GO TO THE LOW, THE FORM OF A MILITARY FORCE IS TO AVOID THE FULL AND ATTACK THE EMPTY; THE FLOW OF WATER IS DETERMINED BY THE EARTH, THE VICTORY OF A MILITARY FORCE IS DETERMINED BY THE OPPONENT.

MASTER SUN

How can you ensure victory if not on the basis of the enemy's own posture? A light brigade cannot hold out long, so if you keep it under siege it will inevitably lose; a heavy brigade will unfailingly respond to a provocation and expose itself. If the opposing army is angry, shame it; if the army is strong, get it to relax. If the opposing general is proud, humiliate him; if the general is greedy, bait him; if the general is suspicious, spy on him right back—therefore the manner of victory is determined according to the enemy.

LI QUAN

SO A MILITARY FORCE HAS NO CONSTANT FORMATION, WATER HAS NO CONSTANT SHAPE: THE ABILITY TO GAIN VICTORY BY CHANGING AND ADAPTING ACCORDING TO THE OPPONENT IS CALLED GENIUS.

MASTER SUN

TSUTSUI JOMYO
AND THE
PRIEST ICHIRAI
ON THE GOJO
BRIDGE,
by Torii
Kiyomasu, 1716.
Spaulding Collection.
Courtesy of the
Museum of Fine
Arts, Boston

SEVEN

ARMED STRUGGLE

Struggle is pursuit of advantage; once emptiness and fullness are determined, one may then struggle with others for advantage.

LI QUAN

Struggle means struggle for advantage; those who get the advantages are thereby victorious. One should first determine whether to use light or heavy arms, and assess whether to approach indirectly or directly, not allowing opponents to take advantage of one's toil.

WANG XI

THE ORDINARY RULE FOR USE OF MILITARY FORCE IS FOR THE MILITARY COMMAND TO RECEIVE THE ORDERS FROM THE CIVILIAN AUTHORITIES, THEN TO GATHER AND MASS THE TROOPS, QUARTERING THEM TOGETHER. NOTHING IS HARDER THAN ARMED STRUGGLE.

MASTER SUN

To fight with people face to face over advantages is the hardest thing in the world.

ZHANG YU

THE DIFFICULTY OF ARMED STRUGGLE IS TO MAKE LONG DISTANCES NEAR AND MAKE PROBLEMS INTO ADVANTAGES.

MASTER SUN

While giving the appearance of being far away, you step up your pace and get there before the opponent.

CAO CAO

Fool opponents into taking it easy, then make haste.

DU MU

MASTER SUN	THEREFORE YOU MAKE THEIR ROUTE A LONG ONE, LURING THEM ON IN HOPES OF GAIN. WHEN YOU SET OUT AFTER OTHERS AND ARRIVE BEFORE THEM, YOU KNOW THE STRATEGY OF MAKING THE DISTANCE NEAR.
JIA LIN	When the opponent really has but a short way to go, if you can lengthen his road by sending him on wild goose chases, you can mislead him so that he cannot come to you to fight.
HO YANXI	You use a special squad to lure the opponent on a wild goose chase, making it seem as though your main force is far away; then you send out a surprise attack force that gets there first, even though it sets out last.
MASTER SUN	THEREFORE ARMED STRUGGLE IS CONSIDERED PROFITABLE, AND ARMED STRUGGLE IS CONSIDERED DANGEROUS.
CAO CAO	For the skilled it is profitable, for the unskilled it is dangerous.
MASTER SUN	TO MOBILIZE THE WHOLE ARMY TO STRUGGLE FOR ADVANTAGE WOULD TAKE TOO LONG, YET TO STRUGGLE FOR ADVANTAGE WITH A STRIPPED-DOWN ARMY RESULTS IN A LACK OF EQUIPMENT. SO IF YOU TRAVEL LIGHT, NOT STOPPING DAY OR NIGHT, DOUBLING YOUR USUAL PACE, STRUGGLING FOR AN ADVANTAGE A HUNDRED MILES AWAY, YOUR MILITARY LEADERS WILL BE CAPTURED. STRONG SOLDIERS WILL GET THERE FIRST, THE WEARY LATER ON—AS A RULE, ONE IN TEN MAKE IT.
JIA LIN	When the road is long the people are weary; if their strength has been used up in travel, then they are worn out while their opponents are fresh, so they are sure to be attacked.
MASTER SUN	STRUGGLING FOR AN ADVANTAGE FIFTY MILES AWAY WILL THWART THE FORWARD LEADERSHIP, AND AS A RULE ONLY FIFTY PERCENT OF THE SOLDIERS MAKE IT. STRUGGLE FOR AN ADVANTAGE THIRTY MILES AWAY, AND TWO OUT OF THREE GET THERE.

SO AN ARMY PERISHES IF IT HAS NO EQUIPMENT, IT PERISHES IF IT HAS NO FOOD, AND IT PERISHES IF IT HAS NO MONEY.

MEI YAOCHEN

These three things are necessary—you cannot fight to win with an unequipped army.

MASTER SUN

SO IF YOU DO NOT KNOW THE PLANS OF YOUR COMPETITORS, YOU CANNOT MAKE INFORMED ALLIANCES.

CAO CAO

You cannot make alliances unless you know the conditions, feelings, and plans of opponents.

DU MU

No, this means that you have to know competitors' plans before you can fight with them. If you don't know their strategy, you should certainly not do battle with them.

CHEN HAO

Both explanations make sense.

MASTER SUN

UNLESS YOU KNOW THE MOUNTAINS AND FORESTS, THE DEFILES AND IMPASSES, AND THE LAY OF THE MARSHES AND SWAMPS, YOU CANNOT MANEUVER WITH AN ARMED FORCE. UNLESS YOU USE LOCAL GUIDES, YOU CANNOT GET THE ADVANTAGES OF THE LAND.

LI QUAN

When you go into enemy territory, you need local people to guide you along the most convenient routes, lest you be hemmed in by mountains and rivers, get bogged down on swampy ground, or lack access to springs and wells. This is what the *I Ching* means when it says, "Chasing deer without a guide only takes you into the bush."

ZHANG YU

Only when you know every detail of the lay of the land can you maneuver and contend.

MEI YAOCHEN

Local guides can be captured or recruited, but it is best to have developed professional scouts, who need not be people of a specific area.

MASTER SUN

SO A MILITARY FORCE IS ESTABLISHED BY DECEPTION, MOBILIZED BY GAIN, AND ADAPTED BY DIVISION AND COMBINATION.

DU MU   A military force is established by deception in the sense that you deceive enemies so that they do not know your real condition, and then can establish supremacy. It is mobilized by gain in the sense that it goes into action when it sees an advantage. Dividing and recombining is done to confuse opponents and observe how they react to you, so that then you can adapt in such a way as to seize victory.

MASTER SUN   THEREFORE WHEN IT MOVES SWIFTLY IT IS LIKE THE WIND, WHEN IT GOES SLOWLY IT IS LIKE A FOREST; IT IS RAPACIOUS AS FIRE, IMMOVABLE AS MOUNTAINS.

LI QUAN

It is swift as the wind in that it comes without a trace and withdraws like lightning. It is like a forest in that it is orderly. It is rapacious as fire across a plain, not leaving a single blade of grass. It is immovable as a mountain when it garrisons.

WANG XI   It is swift as the wind in the speed with which it rushes into openings.

DU MU   It is so fiery and fierce that none can stand up to it.

JIA LIN   When it sees no advantage in action, it remains immovable as a mountain, even though opponents try to lure it out.

MASTER SUN   IT IS AS HARD TO KNOW AS THE DARK; ITS MOVEMENT IS LIKE PEALING THUNDER.

MEI YAOCHEN   Hard to know as the dark means being unobtrusive and inscrutable. Moving like thunder means being so fast no one can get out of your way.

HO YANXI   You conceal your strategy in order to be able to exert this much energy all at once.

MASTER SUN   TO PLUNDER A LOCALITY, DIVIDE UP YOUR TROOPS. TO EXPAND YOUR TERRITORY, DIVIDE THE SPOILS.

The rule for military operations is to feed off the enemy as much as possible. However, in localities where people do not have very much, it is necessary to divide up the troops into smaller groups to take what they need here and there, for only then will there be enough.

As for dividing the spoils, this means it is necessary to divide up the troops to guard what has been gained, not letting enemies get it. Some say it means that when you get land you divide it among those who helped you get it, but in this context I suspect this is not what is meant.

ZHANG YU

ACT AFTER HAVING MADE ASSESSMENTS. THE ONE WHO FIRST KNOWS THE MEASURES OF FAR AND NEAR WINS—THIS IS THE RULE OF ARMED STRUGGLE.

MASTER SUN

The first to move is the guest, the last to move is the host. The guest has it hard, the host has it easy. Far and near means travel—fatigue, hunger, and cold arise from travel.

LI QUAN

AN ANCIENT BOOK OF MILITARY ORDER SAYS, "WORDS ARE NOT HEARD, SO CYMBALS AND DRUMS ARE MADE. OWING TO LACK OF VISIBILITY, BANNERS AND FLAGS ARE MADE." CYMBALS, DRUMS, BANNERS AND FLAGS ARE USED TO FOCUS AND UNIFY PEOPLE'S EARS AND EYES. ONCE PEOPLE ARE UNIFIED, THE BRAVE CANNOT PROCEED ALONE, THE TIMID CANNOT RETREAT ALONE—THIS IS THE RULE FOR EMPLOYING A GROUP.

MASTER SUN

To unify people's ears and eyes means to make people look and listen in concert so that they do not become confused and disorderly. Signals are used to indicate directions and prevent individuals from going off by themselves.

MEI YAOCHEN

SO IN NIGHT BATTLES YOU USE MANY FIRES AND DRUMS, IN DAYTIME BATTLES YOU USE MANY BANNERS AND FLAGS, SO AS TO MANIPULATE PEOPLE'S EARS AND EYES.

MASTER SUN

Have your soldiers adapt their movements according to your signals.

DU MU

MEI YAOCHEN	The reason you use many signals is to manipulate and confuse the perceptions of enemies.
WANG XI	You use many signals to startle their perceptions and make them fear your awesome martial power.
MASTER SUN	SO YOU SHOULD TAKE AWAY THE ENERGY OF THEIR ARMIES, AND TAKE AWAY THE HEART OF THEIR GENERALS.
ZHANG YU	Energy is what battle depends on. Any living thing can be stirred to fight, but even those who fight without regard for death are the way they are because their energy compels them to be that way. Therefore the rule for military operations is that if you can stir up the soldiers of all ranks with a common anger, then no one can stand up to them. Therefore, when opponents first come and their energy is keen, you break this down by not fighting with them for the time being. Watch for when they slump into boredom, then strike, and their keen energy can be taken away.
	As for taking away the heart of their generals, the heart is the ruler of the general—order and disorder, courage and timidity, all are based on the mind. So those skilled in controlling opponents stir them into disorder, incite them to confusion, press them into fear—thus can the schemes in their hearts be taken away.
HO YANXI	First you must be capable of firmness in your own heart—only then can you take away the heart of opposing generals. This is why tradition says that people of former times had the heart to take away hearts, and the ancient law of charioteers says that when the basic mind is firm, fresh energy is victorious.
MASTER SUN	SO MORNING ENERGY IS KEEN, MIDDAY ENERGY SLUMPS, EVENING ENERGY RECEDES—THEREFORE THOSE SKILLED IN USE OF ARMS AVOID THE KEEN ENERGY AND STRIKE THE SLUMPING AND RECEDING. THESE ARE THOSE WHO MASTER ENERGY.
MEI YAOCHEN	The morning means the beginning, midday means the middle, and the evening means the end. What this says is that soldiers are keen at first,

SOLDIERS ON HORSEBACK. Ming dynasty, 1368–1644

but eventually they slump and think of going home, so at this point they are vulnerable.

HO YANXI   Everyone likes security and dislikes danger, everyone wants to live and fears death—so if you chase them to death's door for no reason, making them glad to go to battle, it must be because they have angry and contentious energy in their hearts that has temporarily been taken advantage of to stir them into such a state that they go into danger and imperil themselves without concern or trepidation. Invariably they will regret this and shrink back in fear. Now any weakling in the world will fight in a minute if he gets excited, but when it comes to actually taking up arms and seeking to do battle, this is being possessed by energy—when this energy wanes they will stop, get frightened, and feel regret. The reason that armies look upon strong enemies the way they look at virgin girls is that their aggressiveness is being taken advantage of, as they are stirred up over something.

MASTER SUN   USING ORDER TO DEAL WITH THE DISORDERLY, USING CALM TO DEAL WITH THE CLAMOROUS, IS MASTERING THE HEART.

DU MU   Once your basic mind is settled, you should just tune and order it, making it calm and stable, undisturbed by events, not deluded by prospects of gain. Watch for disorder and clamor among the enemy ranks, then attack.

HO YANXI   A general, with only one body and one heart, leads a million troops to face fierce enemies—gain and loss, victory and defeat, are intermixed; strategy and intelligence change ten thousand times—and this is placed in the general's chest. So unless your heart is wide open and your mind is orderly, you cannot be expected to be able to adapt responsively without limit, dealing with events unerringly, facing great and unexpected difficulties without upset, calmly handling everything without confusion.

MASTER SUN   STANDING YOUR GROUND AWAITING THOSE FAR AWAY, AWAITING THE WEARY IN COMFORT, AWAITING THE HUNGRY WITH FULL STOMACHS, IS MASTERING STRENGTH.

TAMONTEN
(VAISRAVAN
circa 1188–8

LI QUAN	This refers to the forces of guest and host.
DU MU	This is what is meant by getting others to come to you while avoiding being induced to go to others.
MASTER SUN	AVOIDING CONFRONTATION WITH ORDERLY RANKS AND NOT ATTACKING GREAT FORMATIONS IS MASTERING ADAPTATION.
HO YANXI	This is what was earlier referred to as avoiding the strong.
MASTER SUN	SO THE RULE FOR MILITARY OPERATIONS IS NOT TO FACE A HIGH HILL AND NOT TO OPPOSE THOSE WITH THEIR BACKS TO A HILL.
DU MU	This means that when opponents are on high ground you shouldn't attack upward, and when they are charging downward you shouldn't oppose them.
MASTER SUN	DO NOT FOLLOW A FEIGNED RETREAT. DO NOT ATTACK CRACK TROOPS.
JIA LIN	If opponents suddenly run away before their energy has faded, there are surely ambushes lying in wait to attack your forces, so you should carefully restrain your officers from pursuit.
LI QUAN	Avoid strong energy. Mei Yaochen added, "Watch for the energy to crumble."
MASTER SUN	DO NOT EAT FOOD FOR THEIR SOLDIERS.
DU MU	If the enemy suddenly abandon their food supplies, they should be tested first before eating, lest they be poisoned.
MASTER SUN	DO NOT STOP AN ARMY ON ITS WAY HOME.
LI QUAN	When soldiers want to go home, their will cannot be thwarted.

Under these circumstances, an opponent will fight to the death.　　MEI YAOCHEN

A SURROUNDED ARMY MUST BE GIVEN A WAY OUT.　　MASTER SUN

The ancient rule of the charioteers says, "Surround them on three sides, leaving one side open, to show them a way to life."　　CAO CAO

Show them a way to life so that they will not be in the mood to fight to the death, and then you can take advantage of this to strike them.　　DU MU

DO NOT PRESS A DESPERATE ENEMY. 　　MASTER SUN

An exhausted animal will still fight, as a matter of natural law.　　MEI YAOCHEN

If the opponents burn their boats, destroy their cooking pots, and come to fight it out once and for all, don't press them, for when animals are desperate they thrash about wildly.　　ZHANG YU

THESE ARE RULES OF MILITARY OPERATIONS.　　MASTER SUN

THE PATTERN OF CHANGE. Taoist talismanic diagram

EIGHT

ADAPTATIONS

Adaptation means not clinging to fixed methods, but changing appropriately according to events, acting as is suitable.

ZHANG YU

THE GENERAL RULE FOR MILITARY OPERATIONS IS THAT THE MILITARY LEADERSHIP RECEIVES THE ORDER FROM THE CIVILIAN LEADERSHIP TO GATHER ARMIES.

MASTER SUN

LET THERE BE NO ENCAMPMENT ON DIFFICULT TERRAIN. LET NO DIPLOMATIC RELATIONS BE ESTABLISHED AT BORDERS. DO NOT STAY IN BARREN OR ISOLATED TERRITORY.

WHEN ON SURROUNDED GROUND, PLOT. WHEN ON DEADLY GROUND, FIGHT.

Being on surrounded ground means there is steep terrain on all sides, with you in the middle, so that the enemy can come and go freely but you have a hard time getting out and back. When you are on ground like this, you should set up special plans ahead of time to prevent the enemy from bothering you, thus balancing out the disadvantage of the ground.

JIA LIN

Place an army in a deadly situation and the soldiers will make it their own fight.

LI QUAN

THERE ARE ROUTES NOT TO BE FOLLOWED, ARMIES NOT TO BE

MASTER SUN

ATTACKED, CITADELS NOT TO BE BESIEGED, TERRITORY NOT TO BE FOUGHT OVER, ORDERS OF CIVILIAN GOVERNMENTS NOT TO BE OBEYED.

LI QUAN

If there are narrow straits along the way and there may be ambush attacks, that road should not be taken.

DU MU

Don't attack crack troops, don't try to stop a returning army, don't press a desperate enemy, don't attack a ground of death. And if you are strong and the enemy is weak, don't strike their vanguard, lest you frighten the rest into retreating.

CAO CAO

It may be possible to strike an army, but not advisable, because the lay of the land makes it hard to persist, to stay there would mean loss of further gains, present gains would in any case be slight, and a desperate army will fight to the death.

When a citadel is small and secure, and has plenty of supplies, then do not besiege it. When a territory is of marginal benefit and is as easy to lose as it is to win, then don't fight over it. When it is a matter of expediting your work, don't be limited to the commands of the civilian leadership.

DU MU

Wei Liaozi said, "Weapons are instruments of ill omen, conflict is a negative quality, warrior-leaders are officers of death with no heaven above, no earth below, no opponent ahead, no ruler behind."

MASTER SUN

THEREFORE GENERALS WHO KNOW ALL POSSIBLE ADAPTATIONS TO TAKE ADVANTAGE OF THE GROUND KNOW HOW TO USE MILITARY FORCES. IF GENERALS DO NOT KNOW HOW TO ADAPT ADVANTAGEOUSLY, EVEN IF THEY KNOW THE LAY OF THE LAND THEY CANNOT TAKE ADVANTAGE OF IT.

IF THEY RULE ARMIES WITHOUT KNOWING THE ARTS OF COMPLETE ADAPTIVITY, EVEN IF THEY KNOW WHAT THERE IS TO GAIN, THEY CANNOT GET PEOPLE TO WORK FOR THEM.

JIA LIN

Even if you know the configuration of the land, if your mind is inflexible you will not only fail to take advantage of the ground but may even be harmed by it. It is important for generals to adapt in appropriate ways.

If you can change with the momentum of forces, then the advantage does not change, so the only ones who get hurt are others. Therefore there is no constant structure. If you can fully comprehend this principle, you can get people to work.

Adaptation means things like avoiding a convenient route when it is realized that it has features that lend themselves to ambush; not attacking a vulnerable army when it is realized that the army is desperate and bound to fight to the death; not besieging an isolated and vulnerable city when it is realized that it has abundant supplies, powerful weapons, smart generals, and loyal administrators, so there is no telling what might happen; not fighting over territory that could be contested when it is realized that even if it were won it would be hard to keep, it would be of no use anyway, and it would cost people life and limb; not following the directives of the civilian government, which ordinarily should be followed, when it is realized that there would be disadvantage and consequent harm in direction from behind the lines.

These adaptations are made on the spot as appropriate, and cannot be fixed in advance.

Greed for what can be gained means taking any shortcut, attacking any isolated army, besieging any insecure city, contesting any territory that can be taken, taking command of any serviceable army. If you are greedy for what you can get from these things and do not know how to adapt to changes such as outlined above, not only will you be unable to get people to work, you will destroy the army and wound the soldiers.

THEREFORE THE CONSIDERATIONS OF THE INTELLIGENT ALWAYS IN-CLUDE BOTH BENEFIT AND HARM. AS THEY CONSIDER BENEFIT, THEIR WORK CAN EXPAND; AS THEY CONSIDER HARM, THEIR TROUBLES CAN BE RESOLVED.

MASTER SUN

Benefit and harm are interdependent, so the enlightened always consider them.

HO YANXI

NINE DRAGONS (detail) dated 1244, by Chen Rong
Francis Gardner Curtis Fund. Courtesy of the Museum of Fine Arts, Boston

MASTER SUN	THEREFORE WHAT RESTRAINS COMPETITORS IS HARM, WHAT KEEPS COMPETITORS BUSY IS WORK, WHAT MOTIVATES COMPETITORS IS PROFIT.
ZHANG YU	Put them in a vulnerable position and they will surrender on their own. Another strategy is to cause rifts in their ranks, causing harm by wearying them and putting the people out of work.
DU MU	Wear enemies out by keeping them busy and not letting them rest. But you have to have done your own work before you can do this. This work means developing a strong militia, a rich nation, a harmonious society, and an orderly way of life.
MASTER SUN	SO THE RULE OF MILITARY OPERATIONS IS NOT TO COUNT ON OPPONENTS NOT COMING, BUT TO RELY ON HAVING WAYS OF DEALING WITH THEM; NOT TO COUNT ON OPPONENTS NOT ATTACKING, BUT TO RELY ON HAVING WHAT CANNOT BE ATTACKED.
HO YANXI	If you can always remember danger when you are secure and remember chaos in times of order, watch out for danger and chaos while they are still formless and prevent them before they happen, this is best of all.
MASTER SUN	THEREFORE THERE ARE FIVE TRAITS THAT ARE DANGEROUS IN GENERALS: THOSE WHO ARE READY TO DIE CAN BE KILLED; THOSE WHO ARE INTENT ON LIVING CAN BE CAPTURED; THOSE WHO ARE QUICK TO ANGER CAN BE SHAMED; THOSE WHO ARE PURITANICAL CAN BE DISGRACED; THOSE WHO LOVE PEOPLE CAN BE TROUBLED.
CAO CAO	Those who are brave but thoughtless and insist on fighting to the death cannot be made to yield, but they can be struck by ambush.
MENG SHI	When the general is timid and weak and intent on getting back alive, his heart is not really in the battle and his soldiers are not really keen. Both officers and troops are hesitant, so they are vulnerable to attack and capture.

Quick-tempered people can be lured into coming to you by anger and embarrassment, puritanical people can be lured into coming to you by slander and disgrace. And if you appear in a place they are sure to rush to defend, those who love the people there will invariably hasten there to rescue them, troubling and wearying themselves in the process.

THESE FIVE THINGS ARE FAULTS IN GENERALS, DISASTERS FOR MILITARY OPERATIONS.

Good generals are otherwise: they are not committed to death yet do not expect to live; they act in accord with events, not quick to anger, not subject to embarrassment. When they see possibility, they are like tigers, otherwise they shut their doors. Their action and inaction are matters of strategy, and they cannot be pleased or angered.

MANEUVERING ARMIES

This means choosing the most advantageous ways to go.

CAO CAO

WHENEVER YOU STATION AN ARMY TO OBSERVE AN OPPONENT, CUT OFF THE MOUNTAINS AND STAY BY THE VALLEYS.

MASTER SUN

Cutting off the mountains means guarding the defiles, and staying by the valleys means being close to water and fodder.

LI QUAN

WATCH THE LIGHT, STAY ON THE HEIGHTS. WHEN FIGHTING ON A HILL, DO NOT CLIMB. THIS APPLIES TO AN ARMY IN THE MOUNTAINS.

MASTER SUN

One version says, "Fight going down, not climbing up."

DU MU

WHEN CUT OFF BY WATER, ALWAYS STAY AWAY FROM THE WATER. DO NOT MEET THEM IN THE WATER; IT IS ADVANTAGEOUS TO LET HALF OF THEM CROSS AND THEN ATTACK THEM.

MASTER SUN

You induce the enemy to cross over.

CAO CAO AND
LI QUAN

WHEN YOU WANT TO FIGHT, DO NOT FACE AN ENEMY NEAR WATER. WATCH THE LIGHT, STAY IN HIGH PLACES, DO NOT FACE THE CURRENT OF THE WATER. THIS APPLIES TO AN ARMY ON WATER.

MASTER SUN

JIA LIN	In a river basin your armies can be flooded out, and poison can be put in the streams. Facing the current means heading against the flow.
DU MU	It also means your boats should not be moored downstream, lest the enemy ride the current right over you.
MASTER SUN	GO RIGHT THROUGH SALT MARSHES, JUST GO QUICKLY AND DO NOT TARRY. IF YOU RUN INTO AN ARMY IN THE MIDDLE OF A SALT MARSH, STAY BY THE WATERPLANTS, WITH YOUR BACK TO THE TREES. THIS APPLIES TO AN ARMY IN A SALT MARSH.
WANG XI	Should you unexpectedly encounter an opponent in such a situation, here too you should take to the most advantageous factors, with your backs toward the most secure direction.
MASTER SUN	ON A LEVEL PLATEAU, TAKE UP POSITIONS WHERE IT IS EASY TO MANEUVER, KEEPING HIGHER LAND TO YOUR RIGHT REAR, WITH LOW GROUND IN FRONT AND HIGH GROUND BEHIND. THIS APPLIES TO AN ARMY ON A PLATEAU.
DU MU	The warrior-emperor Taigong said, "An army must keep rivers and marshes to the left and hills to the right."
MEI YAOCHEN	Choose level ground, convenient for vehicles; keep hills to your right rear, and you will have a way of getting momentum. It is convenient for fighters if they are heading downhill.
MASTER SUN	IT WAS BY TAKING ADVANTAGE OF THE SITUATION IN THESE FOUR BASIC WAYS THAT THE YELLOW EMPEROR OVERCAME FOUR LORDS.
ZHANG YU	All martial arts began with the Yellow Emperor [a Taoist ruler of late prehistoric times, ca. 2400 B.C.E.], so he is mentioned here.
MASTER SUN	ORDINARILY, AN ARMY LIKES HIGH PLACES AND DISLIKES LOW GROUND, VALUES LIGHT AND DESPISES DARKNESS.

High places are exhilarating, so people are comfortable, and they are also convenient for the force of momentum. Low ground is damp, which promotes illnesses, and makes it hard to fight.

MEI YAOCHEN

When people spend a long time in dark and wet places, they become depressed and ill.

WANG XI

TAKE CARE OF PHYSICAL HEALTH AND STAY WHERE THERE ARE PLENTY OF RESOURCES. WHEN THERE IS NO SICKNESS IN THE ARMY, IT IS SAID TO BE INVINCIBLE.

MASTER SUN

Those who know these things can be certain of victory by the force of their momentum.

MEI YAOCHEN

WHERE THERE ARE HILLS OR EMBANKMENTS KEEP ON THEIR SUNNY SIDE, WITH THEM TO YOUR RIGHT REAR. THIS IS AN ADVANTAGE TO A MILITARY FORCE, THE HELP OF THE LAND.

MASTER SUN

Advantage in a military operation is getting help from the land.

ZHANG YU

WHEN IT RAINS UPSTREAM AND FROTH IS COMING DOWN ON THE CURRENT, IF YOU WANT TO CROSS, WAIT UNTIL IT SETTLES.

MASTER SUN

This is lest the river suddenly swell when you are half across.

CAO CAO

WHENEVER THE TERRAIN HAS IMPASSABLE RAVINES, NATURAL ENCLO-SURES, NATURAL PRISONS, NATURAL TRAPS, NATURAL PITFALLS, AND NATURAL CLEFTS, YOU SHOULD LEAVE QUICKLY AND NOT GET NEAR THEM. FOR MYSELF, I KEEP AWAY FROM THESE, SO THAT OPPONENTS ARE NEARER TO THEM; I KEEP MY FACE TO THESE SO THAT OPPO-NENTS HAVE THEIR BACKS TO THEM.

MASTER SUN

In military operations, always keep away from these six kinds of dangerous ground formation, while maneuvering so that your enemy is near them, with his back to them. Then you have the advantage, and he is out of luck.

CAO CAO

MASTER SUN	WHEN AN ARMY IS TRAVELING, IF THERE IS HILLY TERRITORY WITH MANY STREAMS AND PONDS OR DEPRESSIONS OVERGROWN WITH REEDS, OR WILD FORESTS WITH A LUXURIANT GROWTH OF PLANTS AND TREES, IT IS IMPERATIVE TO SEARCH THEM CAREFULLY AND THOROUGHLY. FOR THESE AFFORD STATIONS FOR BUSHWHACKERS AND SPOILERS.
ZHANG YU	It is imperative to dismount and search, lest there be ambush troops hiding in such places. Also, there is concern that spies might be lurking there watching you and listening to your directives.
MASTER SUN	WHEN THE ENEMY IS NEAR BUT STILL, HE IS RESTING ON A NATURAL STRONGHOLD. WHEN HE IS FAR AWAY BUT TRIES TO PROVOKE HOSTILITIES, HE WANTS YOU TO MOVE FORWARD. IF HIS POSITION IS ACCESSIBLE, IT IS BECAUSE THAT IS ADVANTAGEOUS TO HIM.
DU MU	What this means is that if an opponent does not keep a position on a natural stronghold but stations himself in a convenient place, it must be because there is some practical advantage in doing so.
MASTER SUN	WHEN THE TREES MOVE, THE ENEMY IS COMING; WHEN THERE ARE MANY BLINDS IN THE UNDERGROWTH, IT IS MISDIRECTION.
DU YOU	The idea of making many blinds in the underbrush is to make you think there might be bushwhackers hidden behind them.
MASTER SUN	IF BIRDS START UP, THERE ARE AMBUSHERS THERE. IF THE ANIMALS ARE FRIGHTENED, THERE ARE ATTACKERS THERE. IF DUST RISES HIGH AND SHARP, VEHICLES ARE COMING; IF IT IS LOW AND WIDE, FOOT-SOLDIERS ARE COMING. SCATTERED WISPS OF SMOKE INDICATE WOODCUTTERS. RELATIVELY SMALL AMOUNTS OF DUST COMING AND GOING INDICATE SETTING UP CAMP.
MEI YAOCHEN	Light troops set up camp, so the dust raised by their comings and goings is relatively little.

THOSE WHOSE WORDS ARE HUMBLE WHILE THEY INCREASE WAR PREPARATIONS ARE GOING TO ADVANCE. THOSE WHOSE WORDS ARE STRONG AND WHO ADVANCE AGGRESSIVELY ARE GOING TO RETREAT.

MASTER SUN

If his emissaries come with humble words, send spies to observe him and you will find that the enemy is increasing his preparations.

CAO CAO

When emissaries come with strong words, and their army also moves ahead, they want to threaten you, seeking to retreat.

ZHANG YU

Their words are strong and their posture is aggressive, so you won't think they're going to go away.

WANG XI

WHEN LIGHT VEHICLES COME OUT FIRST AND STAY TO THE SIDES, THEY ARE GOING TO SET UP A BATTLE LINE.

MASTER SUN

They are arraying the troops to do battle.

CAO CAO

The light vehicles establish the boundaries of the battle line.

DU MU

THOSE WHO COME SEEKING PEACE WITHOUT A TREATY ARE PLOTTING.

MASTER SUN

Seeking peace without a treaty is a general statement about cases where countries have been behaving aggressively toward each other, with neither giving in, then all of a sudden one of them comes seeking peace and friendship for no apparent reason. It must be that some internal crisis has arisen, and one side wants a temporary peace to take care of its own problems. Otherwise, it must be that they know you have power that can be used, and they want to make you unsuspecting, so they take the initiative in seeking peace and friendship, thereafter taking advantage of your lack of preparation to come and take over.

CHEN HAO

THOSE WHO BUSILY SET OUT ARRAYS OF ARMED VEHICLES ARE EXPECTING REINFORCEMENTS.

MASTER SUN

Overleaf: ROYAL PROCESSION TO THE CITY OF HWASONG. Eighteenth century

JIA LIN	They wouldn't rush around for an ordinary rendezvous—there must be a distant force expected at a certain time, when they will join forces to come and attack you. It is best to prepare for this right away.
MASTER SUN	IF HALF THEIR FORCE ADVANCES AND HALF RETREATS, THEY ARE TRYING TO LURE YOU.
DU MU	They feign confusion and disorder to lure you into moving forward.
MASTER SUN	IF THEY BRACE THEMSELVES AS THEY STAND, THEY ARE STARVING. WHEN THOSE SENT TO DRAW WATER FIRST DRINK THEMSELVES, THEY ARE THIRSTY.
ZHANG YU	People lose their energy when they do not eat, so they brace themselves on their weapons to stand up. Since all the men in an army eat at the same time, if one is starving all are starving.
WANG XI	By these you can see their ranks are pursued by hunger and thirst.
MASTER SUN	WHEN THEY SEE AN ADVANTAGE BUT DO NOT ADVANCE ON IT, THEY ARE WEARY.
ZHANG YU	When the officers and soldiers are tired out, they cannot be made to fight, so even if they see an advantage to be gained, the generals do not dare to proceed.
MASTER SUN	IF BIRDS ARE GATHERED THERE, THE PLACE HAS BEEN VACATED.
LI QUAN	If there are birds on a citadel, the army has fled.
MASTER SUN	IF THERE ARE CALLS IN THE NIGHT, THEY ARE AFRAID.
CAO CAO	When soldiers call in the night, it means the general is not brave.
DU MU	They are fearful and uneasy, so they call to each other to strengthen themselves.

If there is one person in ten with courage, even though the other nine are timid and cowardly, depending on the bravery of that one man they can still be secure. Now if the soldiers call out in the night, it is because the general has no courage, as Cao Cao says.

CHEN HAO

IF THE ARMY IS UNSETTLED, IT MEANS THE GENERAL IS NOT TAKEN SERIOUSLY.

MASTER SUN

If the general lacks authority, the army is disorderly.

LI QUAN

IF SIGNALS MOVE, THAT MEANS THEY ARE IN CONFUSION.

MASTER SUN

Signals are used to unify the group, so if they move about unsteadily, it means the ranks are in disarray.

ZHANG YU

IF THEIR EMISSARIES ARE IRRITABLE, IT MEANS THEY ARE TIRED.

MASTER SUN

People are irritable when they are fatigued.

JIA LIN

WHEN THEY KILL THEIR HORSES FOR MEAT, IT MEANS THAT THE SOL-DIERS HAVE NO FOOD; WHEN THEY HAVE NO POTS AND DO NOT GO BACK TO THEIR QUARTERS, THEY ARE DESPERATE ADVERSARIES.

MASTER SUN

When they kill their horses for food, get rid of their cooking utensils, and stay out in the open, not returning to their quarters, they are desperadoes and will surely fight to the death for victory.

MEI YAOCHEN

WHEN THERE ARE MURMURINGS, LAPSES IN DUTIES, AND EXTENDED CONVERSATIONS, THE LOYALTY OF THE GROUP HAS BEEN LOST.

MASTER SUN

Murmurings means people spitting out their true feelings, lapses in duties means negligence on the job; as for extended conversations, why would the strong fear the alienation of the group?

MEI YAOCHEN

Murmurings describe talk of true feelings, lapses in duties indicate trou-

WANG XI

ble with superiors. When the military leadership has lost the people's loyalty, they talk to each other frankly about the trouble with their superiors.

MASTER SUN   WHEN THEY GIVE OUT NUMEROUS REWARDS, IT MEANS THEY ARE AT AN IMPASSE; WHEN THEY GIVE OUT NUMEROUS PUNISHMENTS, IT MEANS THEY ARE WORN OUT.

DU MU   When the force of their momentum is exhausted, they give repeated rewards to please their soldiers, lest they rebel en masse. When the people are worn out, they do not fear punishment, so they are punished repeatedly so as to terrorize them.

MEI YAOCHEN   When people are so worn out that they cannot carry out orders, they are punished again and again to establish authority.

MASTER SUN   TO BE VIOLENT AT FIRST AND WIND UP FEARING ONE'S PEOPLE IS THE EPITOME OF INEPTITUDE.

LI QUAN   To act inconsiderately and later be afraid is bravery without firmness, which is extremely incompetent.

MASTER SUN   THOSE WHO COME IN A CONCILIATORY MANNER WANT TO REST.

DU YOU   If they come humbly in a conciliatory manner before they have been subdued in battle, it means they want to rest.

WANG XI   Their momentum cannot last long.

MASTER SUN   WHEN FORCES ANGRILY CONFRONT YOU BUT DELAY ENGAGEMENT, YET DO NOT LEAVE, IT IS IMPERATIVE TO WATCH THEM CAREFULLY.

CAO CAO   They are preparing a surprise attack.

MASTER SUN   IN MILITARY MATTERS IT IS NOT NECESSARILY BENEFICIAL TO HAVE MORE STRENGTH, ONLY TO AVOID ACTING AGGRESSIVELY; IT IS

SHUKONGO SHIN
(VAJRAPANI)
circa 1193–1203,
by Kaikei

ENOUGH TO CONSOLIDATE YOUR POWER, ASSESS OPPONENTS, AND GET PEOPLE, THAT IS ALL.

CHEN HAO   When your military power is not greater than that of the enemy, and there is no advantage to move on, it is not necessary to ask for troops from other countries, just to consolidate your power and get people among the local workers—then you can still defeat the enemy.

JIA LIN   A large group striking a small group is not held in high esteem; what is held in high esteem is when a small group can strike a large group.

MASTER SUN   THE INDIVIDUALIST WITHOUT STRATEGY WHO TAKES OPPONENTS LIGHTLY WILL INEVITABLY BECOME THE CAPTIVE OF OTHERS.

DU MU   If you have no ulterior scheme and no forethought, but just rely on your individual bravery, flippantly taking opponents lightly and giving no consideration to the situation, you will surely be taken prisoner.

MASTER SUN   IF SOLDIERS ARE PUNISHED BEFORE A PERSONAL ATTACHMENT TO THE LEADERSHIP IS FORMED, THEY WILL NOT SUBMIT, AND IF THEY DO NOT SUBMIT THEY ARE HARD TO EMPLOY.

WANG XI   If feelings of appreciation and trust are not established in people's minds from the beginning, they will not form this bond.

MASTER SUN   IF PUNISHMENTS ARE NOT EXECUTED AFTER PERSONAL ATTACHMENT HAS BEEN ESTABLISHED WITH THE SOLDIERS, THEN THEY CANNOT BE EMPLOYED.

ZHANG YU   When there are underlying feelings of appreciation and trust, and the hearts of the soldiers are already bonded to the leadership, if punishments are relaxed the soldiers will become haughty and impossible to employ.

MASTER SUN   THEREFORE DIRECT THEM THROUGH CULTURAL ARTS, UNIFY THEM THROUGH MARTIAL ARTS; THIS MEANS CERTAIN VICTORY.

Cultural art means humaneness, martial art means law.   CAO CAO

Cultural art means benevolence and reward, martial art means sternness   LI QUAN
and punishment.

Command them humanely and benevolently, unify them strictly and   MEI YAOCHEN
sternly. When benevolence and sternness are both evident, it is possible
to be sure of victory.

WHEN DIRECTIVES ARE CONSISTENTLY CARRIED OUT TO EDIFY THE   MASTER SUN
POPULACE, THE POPULACE ACCEPTS. WHEN DIRECTIVES ARE NOT
CONSISTENTLY CARRIED OUT TO EDIFY THE POPULACE, THE POPULACE
DOES NOT ACCEPT. WHEN DIRECTIVES ARE CONSISTENTLY CARRIED
OUT, THERE IS MUTUAL SATISFACTION BETWEEN THE LEADERSHIP AND
THE GROUP.

Consistent means all along: in ordinary times it is imperative that bene-   DU MU
olence and trustworthiness along with dignity and order be manifest to
people from the start, so that later, if they are faced with enemies it is
possible to meet the situation in an orderly fashion, with the full trust
and acceptance of the people.

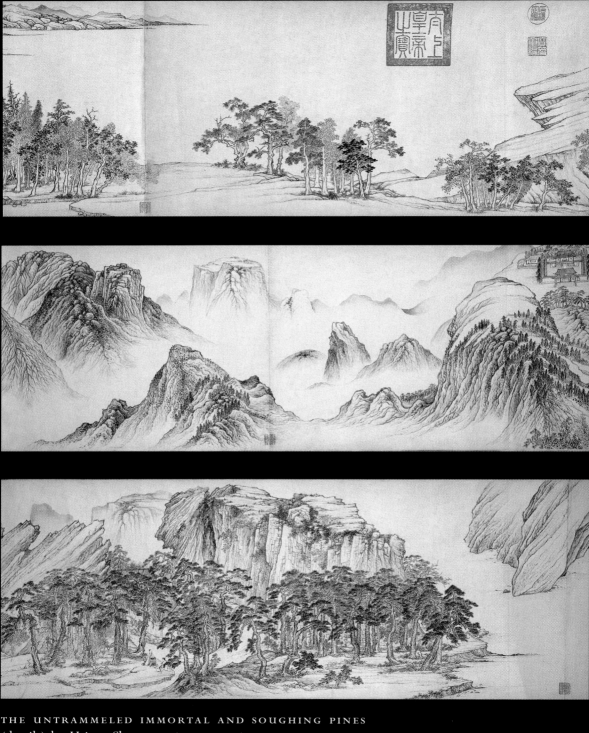

THE UNTRAMMELED IMMORTAL AND SOUGHING PINES
(details) by Hsiang Sheng-mo (1597-1658).
Frederick L. Jack Fund, Courtesy of the Museum of Fine Arts, Boston

TEN

TERRAIN

SOME TERRAIN IS EASILY PASSABLE, IN SOME YOU GET HUNG UP, SOME MAKES FOR A STANDOFF, SOME IS NARROW, SOME IS STEEP, SOME IS WIDE OPEN.

WHEN BOTH SIDES CAN COME AND GO, THE TERRAIN IS SAID TO BE EASILY PASSABLE. WHEN THE TERRAIN IS EASILY PASSABLE, TAKE UP YOUR POSITION FIRST, CHOOSING THE HIGH AND SUNNY SIDE, CONVENIENT TO SUPPLY ROUTES, FOR ADVANTAGE IN BATTLE.

WHEN YOU CAN GO BUT HAVE A HARD TIME GETTING BACK, YOU ARE SAID TO BE HUNG UP. ON THIS TYPE OF TERRAIN, IF THE OPPONENT IS UNPREPARED, YOU WILL PREVAIL IF YOU GO FORTH, BUT IF THE ENEMY IS PREPARED, IF YOU GO FORTH AND DO NOT PREVAIL YOU WILL HAVE A HARD TIME GETTING BACK, TO YOUR DISADVANTAGE.

WHEN IT IS DISADVANTAGEOUS FOR EITHER SIDE TO GO FORTH, IT IS CALLED STANDOFF TERRAIN. ON STANDOFF TERRAIN, EVEN THOUGH THE OPPONENT OFFERS YOU AN ADVANTAGE, YOU DO NOT GO FOR IT—YOU WITHDRAW, INDUCING THE ENEMY HALF OUT, AND THEN YOU ATTACK, TO YOUR ADVANTAGE.

ON NARROW TERRAIN, IF YOU ARE THERE FIRST, YOU SHOULD FILL IT UP TO AWAIT THE OPPONENT. IF THE OPPONENT IS THERE FIRST, DO NOT PURSUE IF THE OPPONENT FILLS THE NARROWS. PURSUE IF THE OPPONENT DOES NOT FILL THE NARROWS.

ON STEEP TERRAIN, IF YOU ARE THERE FIRST, YOU SHOULD OC-

MASTER SUN

CUPY THE HIGH AND SUNNY SIDE TO AWAIT THE OPPONENT. IF THE OPPONENT IS THERE FIRST, WITHDRAW FROM THERE AND DO NOT PURSUE.

ON WIDE-OPEN TERRAIN, THE FORCE OF MOMENTUM IS EQUALIZED, AND IT IS HARD TO MAKE A CHALLENGE, DISADVANTAGEOUS TO FIGHT.

UNDERSTANDING THESE SIX KINDS OF TERRAIN IS THE HIGHEST RESPONSIBILITY OF THE GENERAL, AND IT IS IMPERATIVE TO EXAMINE THEM.

LI QUAN

These are the configurations of terrain; generals who do not know them lose.

MEI YAOCHEN

The form of the land is the basis on which the military is aided and victory is established, so it must be measured.

MASTER SUN

SO AMONG MILITARY FORCES THERE ARE THOSE WHO RUSH, THOSE WHO TARRY, THOSE WHO FALL, THOSE WHO CRUMBLE, THOSE WHO RIOT, AND THOSE WHO GET BEATEN. THESE ARE NOT NATURAL DISASTERS, BUT FAULTS OF THE GENERALS.

THOSE WHO HAVE EQUAL MOMENTUM BUT STRIKE TEN WITH ONE ARE IN A RUSH. THOSE WHOSE SOLDIERS ARE STRONG BUT WHOSE OFFICERS ARE WEAK TARRY. THOSE WHOSE OFFICERS ARE STRONG BUT WHOSE SOLDIERS ARE WEAK FALL. WHEN COLONELS ARE ANGRY AND OBSTREPEROUS AND FIGHT ON THEIR OWN OUT OF SPITE WHEN THEY MEET OPPONENTS, AND THE GENERALS DO NOT KNOW THEIR ABILITIES, THEY CRUMBLE.

ZHANG YU

Generally speaking, the entire military leadership has to be of one mind, all of the military forces have to cooperate, in order to be able to defeat opponents.

MASTER SUN

WHEN THE GENERALS ARE WEAK AND LACK AUTHORITY, INSTRUCTIONS ARE NOT CLEAR, OFFICERS AND SOLDIERS LACK CONSISTENCY, AND THEY FORM BATTLE LINES EVERY WHICH WAY, THIS IS RIOT. WHEN THE GENERALS CANNOT ASSESS OPPONENTS, CLASH WITH

MUCH GREATER NUMBERS OR MORE POWERFUL FORCES, AND DO NOT SORT OUT THE LEVELS OF SKILL AMONG THEIR OWN TROOPS, THESE ARE THE ONES WHO GET BEATEN.

If you employ soldiers without sorting out the skilled and unskilled, the brave and the timid, you are bringing defeat on yourself.

JIA LIN

THESE SIX ARE WAYS TO DEFEAT. UNDERSTANDING THIS IS THE ULTIMATE RESPONSIBILITY OF THE GENERALS; THEY MUST BE EXAMINED.

MASTER SUN

First is not assessing numbers, second is lack of a clear system of punishments and rewards, third is failure in training, forth is irrational overexcitement, fifth is ineffectiveness of law and order, and sixth is failure to choose the strong and resolute.

CHEN HAO

These are ways to certain defeat.

ZHANG YU

THE CONTOUR OF THE LAND IS AN AID TO AN ARMY; SIZING UP OPPONENTS TO DETERMINE VICTORY, ASSESSING DANGERS AND DISTANCES, IS THE PROPER COURSE OF ACTION FOR MILITARY LEADERS. THOSE WHO DO BATTLE KNOWING THESE WILL WIN, THOSE WHO DO BATTLE WITHOUT KNOWING THESE WILL LOSE.

MASTER SUN

Once you know the opponent's conditions, and also know the advantages of the terrain, you can win in battle. If you know neither, you will lose in battle.

ZHANG YU

THEREFORE, WHEN THE LAWS OF WAR INDICATE CERTAIN VICTORY IT IS SURELY APPROPRIATE TO DO BATTLE, EVEN IF THE GOVERNMENT SAYS THERE IS TO BE NO BATTLE. IF THE LAWS OF WAR DO NOT INDICATE VICTORY, IT IS APPROPRIATE NOT TO DO BATTLE, EVEN IF THE GOVERNMENT ORDERS WAR. THUS ONE ADVANCES WITHOUT SEEKING GLORY, RETREATS WITHOUT AVOIDING BLAME, ONLY PROTECTING PEOPLE, TO THE BENEFIT OF THE GOVERNMENT AS WELL, THUS RENDERING VALUABLE SERVICE TO THE NATION.

MASTER SUN

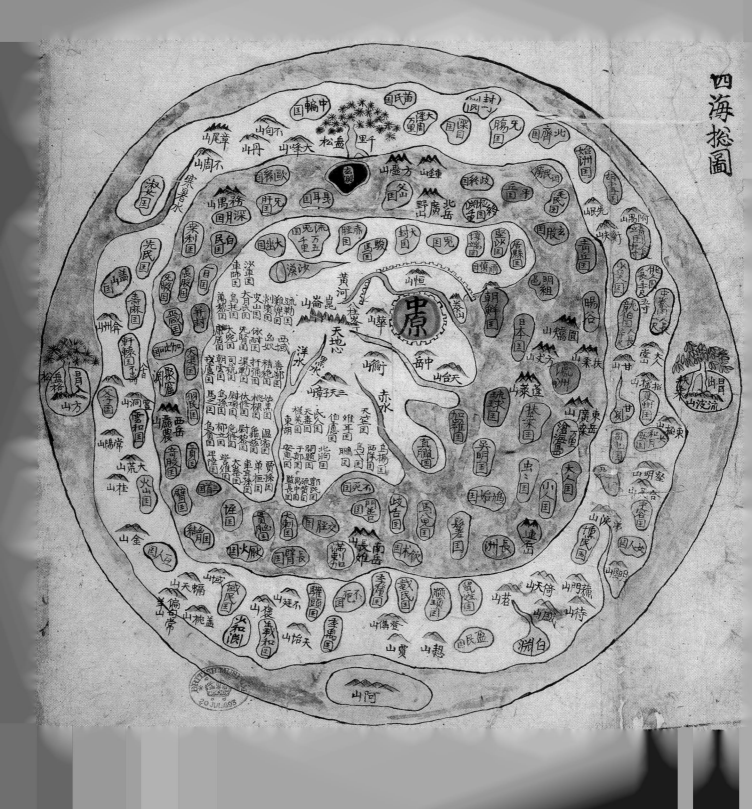

Advancing and retreating contrary to government orders is not done for personal interest, but only to safeguard the lives of the people and accord with the true benefit of the government. Such loyal employees are valuable to a nation.

LOOK UPON YOUR SOLDIERS AS YOU DO INFANTS, AND THEY WILLINGLY GO INTO DEEP VALLEYS WITH YOU; LOOK UPON YOUR SOLDIERS AS BELOVED CHILDREN, AND THEY WILLINGLY DIE WITH YOU.

If you treat them well, you will get their utmost power.

IF YOU ARE SO NICE TO THEM THAT YOU CANNOT EMPLOY THEM, SO KIND TO THEM THAT YOU CANNOT COMMAND THEM, SO CASUAL WITH THEM THAT YOU CANNOT ESTABLISH ORDER, THEY ARE LIKE SPOILED CHILDREN, USELESS.

Rewards should not be used alone, punishments should not be relied on in isolation. Otherwise, like spoiled children, people will become accustomed to either enjoying or resenting everything. This is harmful and renders them useless.

IF YOU KNOW YOUR SOLDIERS ARE CAPABLE OF STRIKING, BUT DO NOT KNOW WHETHER THE ENEMY IS INVULNERABLE TO A STRIKE, YOU HAVE HALF A CHANCE OF WINNING. IF YOU KNOW THE ENEMY IS VULNERABLE TO A STRIKE, BUT DO NOT KNOW IF YOUR SOLDIERS ARE INCAPABLE OF MAKING SUCH A STRIKE, YOU HAVE HALF A CHANCE OF WINNING. IF YOU KNOW THE ENEMY IS VULNERABLE TO A STRIKE, AND KNOW YOUR SOLDIERS CAN MAKE THE STRIKE, BUT DO NOT KNOW IF THE LAY OF THE LAND MAKES IT UNSUITABLE FOR BATTLE, YOU HAVE HALF A CHANCE OF WINNING.

If you know yourself but not the other, or if you know the other but not yourself, in either case you cannot be sure of victory. And even if you know both yourself and your opponent and know you can fight, still you cannot overlook the question of the advantages of the terrain.

STRIDING
INFANTRYMAN
Chin dynasty,
221–206 B.C.E.

THEREFORE THOSE WHO KNOW MARTIAL ARTS DO NOT WANDER WHEN THEY MOVE, AND DO NOT BECOME EXHAUSTED WHEN THEY RISE UP. SO IT IS SAID THAT WHEN YOU KNOW YOURSELF AND OTHERS, VICTORY IS NOT IN DANGER; WHEN YOU KNOW SKY AND EARTH, VICTORY IS INEXHAUSTIBLE.

When victory and defeat are already determined before movement and uprising, you do not become confused in your actions and do not wear yourself out rising up.

When you know what is to others' advantage and what is to your advantage, you are not in danger. When you know the season and the terrain, you do not come to an impasse.

ELEVEN

NINE GROUNDS

ACCORDING TO THE RULE FOR MILITARY OPERATIONS, THERE ARE NINE KINDS OF GROUND. WHERE LOCAL INTERESTS FIGHT AMONG THEMSELVES ON THEIR OWN TERRITORY, THIS IS CALLED A GROUND OF DISSOLUTION.

MASTER SUN

When the soldiers are attached to the land and are near home, they fall apart easily.

CAO CAO

WHEN YOU ENTER OTHERS' LAND, BUT NOT DEEPLY, THIS IS CALLED LIGHT GROUND.

MASTER SUN

This means the soldiers can all get back easily.

CAO CAO

When an army goes forth and crosses a border, it should burn its boats and bridges to show the populace it has no intention of looking back.

DU MU

LAND THAT WOULD BE ADVANTAGEOUS TO YOU IF YOU GOT IT AND TO OPPONENTS IF THEY GOT IT IS CALLED GROUND OF CONTENTION.

MASTER SUN

Ground from which a few could overcome many, the weak could strike the powerful.

CAO CAO

A ground of inevitable contention is any natural barricade or strategic pass.

DU MU

MASTER SUN	LAND WHERE YOU AND OTHERS CAN COME AND GO IS CALLED A TRAFFICKED GROUND.
ZHANG YU	If there are many roads in the area and there is free travel that cannot be cut off, this is what is called a trafficked ground.
MASTER SUN	LAND THAT IS SURROUNDED ON THREE SIDES BY COMPETITORS AND WOULD GIVE THE FIRST TO GET IT ACCESS TO ALL THE PEOPLE ON THE CONTINENT IS CALLED INTERSECTING GROUND.
HO YANXI	Intersecting ground means the intersections of main arteries linking together numerous highway systems: first occupy this ground, and the people will have to go with you. So if you get it you are secure, if you lose it you are in peril.
MASTER SUN	WHEN YOU ENTER DEEPLY INTO OTHERS' LAND, PAST MANY CITIES AND TOWNS, THIS IS CALLED HEAVY GROUND.
CAO CAO	This is ground from which it is hard to return.
MASTER SUN	WHEN YOU TRAVERSE MOUNTAIN FORESTS, STEEP DEFILES, MARSHES, OR ANY ROUTE DIFFICULT TO TRAVEL, THIS IS CALLED BAD GROUND.
HO YANXI	Bad ground is land that lacks stability and is unsuitable for building fortifications and trenches. It is best to leave such terrain as quickly as possible.
MASTER SUN	WHEN THE WAY IN IS NARROW AND THE WAY OUT IS CIRCUITOUS, SO A SMALL ENEMY FORCE CAN STRIKE YOU, EVEN THOUGH YOUR NUMBERS ARE GREATER, THIS IS CALLED SURROUNDED GROUND.
MEI YAOCHEN	If you are capable of extraordinary adaptation, you can travel this ground.
ZHANG YU	On ground that is hemmed in in front and walled off behind, a single defender can hold off a thousand men, so on such ground you win by ambush.

FACE MASK, by Myochin Muneakira, 1673-1745

MASTER SUN   WHEN YOU WILL SURVIVE IF YOU FIGHT QUICKLY AND PERISH IF YOU
DO NOT, THIS IS CALLED DYING GROUND.

CHEN HAO   People on dying ground are, as it were, sitting in a leaking boat, lying
in a burning house.

MEI YAOCHEN   When you cannot press forward, cannot retreat backward, and cannot
run to the sides, you have no choice but to fight right away.

MASTER SUN   SO LET THERE BE NO BATTLE ON A GROUND OF DISSOLUTION, LET
THERE BE NO STOPPING ON LIGHT GROUND, LET THERE BE NO AT-
TACK ON A GROUND OF CONTENTION, LET THERE BE NO CUTTING
OFF OF TRAFFICKED GROUND. ON INTERSECTING GROUND FORM
COMMUNICATIONS, ON HEAVY GROUND PLUNDER, ON BAD GROUND
KEEP GOING, ON SURROUNDED GROUND MAKE PLANS, ON DYING
GROUND FIGHT.

LI QUAN   On a ground of dissolution, the soldiers might run away.

MEI YAOCHEN   Light ground is where soldiers have first entered enemy territory and do
not yet have their backs to the wall; hence the minds of the soldiers are
not really concentrated, and they are not ready for battle. At this point
it is imperative to avoid important cities and highways, and it is advantageous to move quickly onward.

CAO CAO   It is not advantageous to attack an enemy on a ground of contention;
what is advantageous is to get there first.

WANG XI   Trafficked ground should not be cut off, so that the roads may be used
advantageously as supply routes.

MENG SHI   On intersecting ground, if you establish alliances you are safe, if you lose
alliances you are in peril.

CAO CAO   On heavy ground, plundering means building up supplies.
Li Quan added, "When you enter deeply into enemy territory you

should not antagonize people by acting unjustly. When the founder of the great Han dynasty entered the homeland of the supplanted Qin dynasty, there was no rapine or pillage, and this is how he won the people's hearts."

On bad ground, since you cannot entrench, you should make haste to leave there.

LI QUAN

On surrounded ground, bring surprise tactics into play.

CAO CAO

If they fall into dying ground, then everyone in the army will spontaneously fight. This is why it is said, "Put them on dying ground, and then they will live."

CHEN HAO

THOSE WHO ARE CALLED THE GOOD MILITARISTS OF OLD COULD MAKE OPPONENTS LOSE CONTACT BETWEEN FRONT AND BACK LINES, LOSE RELIABILITY BETWEEN LARGE AND SMALL GROUPS, LOSE MUTUAL CONCERN FOR THE WELFARE OF THE DIFFERENT SOCIAL CLASSES AMONG THEM, LOSE MUTUAL ACCOMMODATION BETWEEN THE RULERS AND THE RULED, LOSE ENLISTMENTS AMONG THE SOLDIERS, LOSE COHERENCE WITHIN THE ARMIES. THEY WENT INTO ACTION WHEN IT WAS ADVANTAGEOUS, STOPPED WHEN IT WAS NOT.

MASTER SUN

They set up changes to confuse their opponents, striking them here and there, terrorizing and disarraying them in such a way that they had no time to plan.

LI QUAN

IT MAY BE ASKED, WHEN A LARGE, WELL-ORGANIZED OPPONENT IS ABOUT TO COME TO YOU, HOW DO YOU DEAL WITH IT? THE ANSWER IS THAT YOU FIRST TAKE AWAY WHAT THEY LIKE, AND THEN THEY WILL LISTEN TO YOU.

MASTER SUN

First occupy a position of advantage, and cut off their supply routes by special strike forces, and they will do as you plan.

WANG XI

What they like does not only mean the advantages they rely on, it means that anything enemies care about is worth capturing.

CHEN HAO

MASTER SUN	THE CONDITION OF A MILITARY FORCE IS THAT ITS ESSENTIAL FACTOR IS SPEED, TAKING ADVANTAGE OF OTHERS' FAILURE TO CATCH UP, GOING BY ROUTES THEY DO NOT EXPECT, ATTACKING WHERE THEY ARE NOT ON GUARD.
CHEN HAO	This means that to take advantage of unpreparedness, lack of foresight, or lack of caution on the part of opponents, it is necessary to proceed quickly, it won't work if you hesitate.
MASTER SUN	IN GENERAL, THE PATTERN OF INVASION IS THAT INVADERS BECOME MORE INTENSE THE FARTHER THEY ENTER ALIEN TERRITORY, TO THE POINT WHERE THE NATIVE RULERSHIP CANNOT OVERCOME THEM.
DU MU	The pattern of invasive attack is that if they enter deeply into enemy territory, soldiers come to have the determination to fight to the death—they are singleminded, so the native rulers cannot beat them.
MASTER SUN	GLEAN FROM RICH FIELDS, AND THE ARMIES WILL HAVE ENOUGH TO EAT. TAKE CARE OF YOUR HEALTH AND AVOID STRESS, CONSOLIDATE YOUR ENERGY AND BUILD UP YOUR STRENGTH. MANEUVER YOUR TROOPS AND ASSESS STRATEGIES SO AS TO BE UNFATHOMABLE.
WANG XI	Consolidate your keenest energy, save up your extra strength, keep your form concealed and your plans secret, being unfathomable to enemies, waiting for a vulnerable gap to advance upon.
MASTER SUN	PUT THEM IN A SPOT WHERE THEY HAVE NO PLACE TO GO, AND THEY WILL DIE BEFORE FLEEING. IF THEY ARE TO DIE THERE, WHAT CAN THEY NOT DO? WARRIORS EXERT THEIR FULL STRENGTH. WHEN WARRIORS ARE IN GREAT DANGER, THEN THEY HAVE NO FEAR. WHEN THERE IS NOWHERE TO GO THEY ARE FIRM, WHEN THEY ARE DEEPLY INVOLVED THEY STICK TO IT. IF THEY HAVE NO CHOICE, THEY WILL FIGHT.
CAO CAO	When people are desperate, they will fight to the death.

FOR THIS REASON THE SOLDIERS ARE ALERT WITHOUT BEING DRILLED, ENLIST WITHOUT BEING DRAFTED, ARE FRIENDLY WITHOUT TREATIES, ARE TRUSTWORTHY WITHOUT COMMANDS.

MASTER SUN

This means that when warriors are in mortal danger everyone high and low has the same aim, so they are spontaneously on the alert without being drilled, are spontaneously sympathetic without being drafted, and are spontaneously trustworthy without treaties or commands.

DU MU

PROHIBIT OMENS TO GET RID OF DOUBT, AND SOLDIERS WILL NEVER LEAVE YOU. IF YOUR SOLDIERS HAVE NO EXTRA GOODS, IT IS NOT THAT THEY DISLIKE MATERIAL GOODS. IF THEY HAVE NO MORE LIFE, IT IS NOT THAT THEY DO NOT WANT TO LIVE LONG. ON THE DAY THE ORDER TO MARCH GOES OUT, THE SOLDIERS WEEP.

MASTER SUN

They abandon their goods and go to their death because they have no choice. They weep because they all intend to go to their death.

CAO CAO

If they have valuable possessions, soldiers may become attached to them and lack the spirit to fight to the death, and all are pledged to die.

DU MU

They weep because they are so stirred up.

WANG XI

SO A SKILLFUL MILITARY OPERATION SHOULD BE LIKE A SWIFT SNAKE THAT COUNTERS WITH ITS TAIL WHEN SOMEONE STRIKES AT ITS HEAD, COUNTERS WITH ITS HEAD WHEN SOMEONE STRIKES AT ITS TAIL, AND COUNTERS WITH BOTH HEAD AND TAIL WHEN SOMEONE STRIKES AT ITS MIDDLE.

MASTER SUN

This represents the method of a battle line, responding swiftly when struck. A manual of eight classical battle formations says, "Make the back the front, make the front the back, with four heads and eight tails. Make the head anywhere, and when the enemy lunges into the middle, head and tail both come to the rescue."

ZHANG YU

THE QUESTION MAY BE ASKED, CAN A MILITARY FORCE BE MADE TO

MASTER SUN

BE LIKE THIS SWIFT SNAKE? THE ANSWER IS THAT IT CAN. EVEN PEO-
PLE WHO DISLIKE EACH OTHER, IF IN THE SAME BOAT, WILL HELP
EACH OTHER OUT IN TROUBLE.

MEI YAOCHEN   It is the force of the situation that makes this happen.

MASTER SUN   THEREFORE TETHERED HORSES AND BURIED WHEELS ARE NOT SUFFI-
CIENTLY RELIABLE.

DU MU   Horses are tethered to make a stationary battle line, wheels are buried
to make the vehicles immovable. Even so, this is not sufficiently secure
and reliable. It is necessary to allow adaptation to changes, placing soldiers in deadly situations so that they will fight spontaneously, helping
each other out like two hands—this is the way to security and certain
victory.

MASTER SUN   TO EVEN OUT BRAVERY AND MAKE IT UNIFORM IS THE TAO OF OR-
GANIZATION. TO BE SUCCESSFUL WITH BOTH THE HARD AND SOFT IS
BASED ON THE PATTERN OF THE GROUND.

CHEN HAO   If the orders are strict and clear, the brave cannot advance by themselves
and the timid cannot shrink back by themselves, so the army is like one
man.

ZHANG YU   If you get the advantage of the ground, you can overcome opponents
even with soft, weak troops—how much the more with hard, strong
troops? What makes it possible for both strong and weak to be useful is
the configuration of the ground.

MASTER SUN   THEREFORE THOSE SKILLED IN MILITARY OPERATIONS ACHIEVE COOP-
ERATION IN A GROUP SO THAT DIRECTING THE GROUP IS LIKE DI-
RECTING A SINGLE INDIVIDUAL WITH NO OTHER CHOICE.

DU MU   People having no other choice is a metaphor for the ease with which
they can be directed.

THE BUSINESS OF THE GENERAL IS QUIET AND SECRET, FAIR AND ORDERLY.

MASTER SUN

If you are quiet and inconspicuous, others will not be able to figure you out. If you are accurate and orderly, others will not be able to disturb you.

MEI YAOCHEN

His plans are calm and deeply hidden, so no one can figure them out. His regime is fair and orderly, so no one dares take him lightly.

ZHANG YU

HE CAN KEEP THE SOLDIERS UNAWARE, MAKE THEM IGNORANT.

MASTER SUN

This is because his plans are as yet unripe, and he does not want the soldiers to know them, because it is appropriate to enjoy the final accomplishment with them but not to plan the initial strategy with them.

LI QUAN

This is to make them know nothing but to follow orders, unaware of anything else.

DU MU AND ZHANG YU

HE CHANGES HIS ACTIONS AND REVISES HIS PLANS, SO THAT PEOPLE WILL NOT RECOGNIZE THEM. HE CHANGES HIS ABODE AND GOES BY A CIRCUITOUS ROUTE, SO THAT PEOPLE CANNOT ANTICIPATE HIM.

MASTER SUN

When people never understand what your intention is, then you win. The Great White Mountain Man said, "The reason deception is valued in military operations is not just for deceiving enemies, but to begin with for deceiving one's own troops, to get them to follow unknowingly."

ZHANG YU

WHEN A LEADER ESTABLISHES A GOAL WITH THE TROOPS, HE IS LIKE ONE WHO CLIMBS UP TO A HIGH PLACE AND THEN TOSSES AWAY THE LADDER. WHEN A LEADER ENTERS DEEPLY INTO ENEMY TERRITORY WITH THE TROOPS, HE BRINGS OUT THEIR POTENTIAL. HE HAS THEM BURN THE BOATS AND DESTROY THE POTS, DRIVES THEM LIKE SHEEP, NONE KNOWING WHERE THEY ARE GOING.

MASTER SUN

CAO CAO   He unifies their minds.

LI QUAN   An army that comes back is one that has burned its boats and bridges to
                 make fast its will; since the soldiers do not know the plans, they do not
                 think of looking back either, so they are like herded sheep.

MASTER SUN   TO ASSEMBLE ARMIES AND PUT THEM INTO DANGEROUS SITUATIONS IS
                 THE BUSINESS OF GENERALS. ADAPTATIONS TO DIFFERENT GROUNDS,
                 ADVANTAGES OF CONTRACTION AND EXPANSION, PATTERNS OF HU-
                 MAN FEELINGS AND CONDITIONS—THESE MUST BE EXAMINED.

DU MU   When he talks about the advantages and disadvantages of contraction and
                 expansion, he means that the ordinary patterns of human feelings all
                 change according to the various types of ground.

MASTER SUN   GENERALLY, THE WAY IT IS WITH INVADERS IS THAT THEY UNITE
                 WHEN DEEP IN ENEMY TERRITORY BUT ARE PRONE TO DISSOLVE
                 WHILE ON THE FRINGES. WHEN YOU LEAVE YOUR COUNTRY AND
                 CROSS THE BORDER ON A MILITARY OPERATION, THAT IS ISOLATED
                 GROUND. WHEN IT IS ACCESSIBLE FROM ALL DIRECTIONS, IT IS
                 TRAFFICKED GROUND. WHEN PENETRATION IS DEEP, THAT IS HEAVY
                 GROUND. WHEN PENETRATION IS SHALLOW, THAT IS LIGHT
                 GROUND. WHEN YOUR BACK IS TO AN IMPASSABLE FASTNESS AND
                 BEFORE YOU ARE NARROW STRAITS, THAT IS SURROUNDED
                 GROUND. WHEN THERE IS NOWHERE TO GO, THAT IS DEADLY
                 GROUND.
                     SO ON A GROUND OF DISSOLUTION, I WOULD UNIFY THE
                 MINDS OF THE TROOPS. ON LIGHT GROUND, I WOULD HAVE THEM
                 KEEP IN TOUCH. ON A GROUND OF CONTENTION, I WOULD HAVE
                 THEM FOLLOW UP QUICKLY. ON AN INTERSECTING GROUND, I
                 WOULD BE CAREFUL ABOUT DEFENSE. ON A TRAFFICKED GROUND,
                 I WOULD MAKE ALLIANCES FIRM. ON HEAVY GROUND, I WOULD
                 ENSURE CONTINUOUS SUPPLIES. ON BAD GROUND, I WOULD URGE
                 THEM ONWARD. ON SURROUNDED GROUND, I WOULD CLOSE UP
                 THE GAPS. ON DEADLY GROUND, I WOULD INDICATE TO THEM
                 THERE IS NO SURVIVING.

SO THE PSYCHOLOGY OF SOLDIERS IS TO RESIST WHEN SUR-
ROUNDED, FIGHT WHEN IT CANNOT BE AVOIDED, AND OBEY IN
EXTREMES.

Not until soldiers are surrounded do they each have the determination   DU MU
to resist the enemy and sustain victory. When they are desperate, they
put up a united defense.

When they are fallen into dire straits, they obey completely.   MENG SHI

THEREFORE THOSE WHO DO NOT KNOW THE PLANS OF COMPETITORS   MASTER SUN
CANNOT PREPARE ALLIANCES. THOSE WHO DO NOT KNOW THE LAY
OF THE LAND CANNOT MANEUVER THEIR FORCES. THOSE WHO DO
NOT USE LOCAL GUIDES CANNOT TAKE ADVANTAGE OF THE GROUND.
THE MILITARY OF AN EFFECTIVE RULERSHIP MUST KNOW ALL THESE
THINGS.
    WHEN THE MILITARY OF AN EFFECTIVE RULERSHIP ATTACKS A
LARGE COUNTRY, THE PEOPLE CANNOT UNITE. WHEN ITS POWER
OVERWHELMS OPPONENTS, ALLIANCES CANNOT COME TOGETHER.

If you are able to find out opponents' plans, take advantage of the   WANG XI
ground, and maneuver opponents so that they are helpless, then even a
large country cannot assemble enough people to stop you.

If you rely on the force of wealth and strength to hastily attack a large   ZHANG YU
country, your own people will resent the suffering this causes and will
not unite behind you. If you pose an overwhelming military threat to ri-
val nations, their leaders will fear you and not dare to form alliances.

THEREFORE IF YOU DO NOT COMPETE FOR ALLIANCES ANYWHERE, DO   MASTER SUN
NOT FOSTER AUTHORITY ANYWHERE, BUT JUST EXTEND YOUR PER-
SONAL INFLUENCE, THREATENING OPPONENTS, THIS MAKES TOWN
AND COUNTRY VULNERABLE.

If you do not compete for allies and helpers, then you will be isolated,   ZHANG YU
with little help. If you do not foster your authority, then people will

leave and the country will weaken. If you lash out in personal rage, threatening neighbors with violence, then in the end you bring destruction on yourself.

Another interpretation is that if an enemy country cannot unite its people and assemble its troops, and its alliances cannot come together, then you should cut off its relations and take away its authority, so that you can extend your desires and awe your enemies, so that their citadels can be taken and their countries overthrown.

MASTER SUN   GIVE OUT REWARDS THAT ARE NOT IN THE RULES, GIVE OUT DIRECTIVES THAT ARE NOT IN THE CODE.

MEI YAOCHEN   Consider the merit to give the reward, without rules set up beforehand; observe the opponent to make promises, without prior setup of codes.

JIA LIN   When you want to take a citadel and overthrow a nation, you establish punishments and rewards outside your country, and carry out directives outside your government, so you do not stick to your ordinary rules and codes.

MASTER SUN   EMPLOY THE ENTIRE ARMED FORCES LIKE EMPLOYING A SINGLE PERSON. EMPLOY THEM WITH ACTUAL TASKS, DO NOT TALK TO THEM. MOTIVATE THEM WITH BENEFITS, DO NOT TELL THEM ABOUT HARM.

MEI YAOCHEN   Just employ them to fight, don't tell them your strategy. Let them know what benefit there is in it for them, don't tell them about the potential harm.

WANG XI   If the truth leaks out, your strategy will be foiled. If the soldiers worry, they will be hesitant and fearful.

ZHANG YU   Human psychology is to go for perceived benefits and try to avoid prospective harm.

MASTER SUN   CONFRONT THEM WITH ANNIHILATION, AND THEY WILL THEN SURVIVE; PLUNGE THEM INTO A DEADLY SITUATION, AND THEY WILL

DUKE WEN OF CHIN RECOVERING HIS STATE (detail),
by Li T'ang, circa 1070–1150

THEN LIVE. WHEN PEOPLE FALL INTO DANGER, THEY ARE THEN ABLE TO STRIVE FOR VICTORY.

MEI YAOCHEN
Until they are trapped on difficult ground, soldiers are not fully concentrated in mind; once they have fallen into danger and difficulty, then the question of winning or losing depends on what people do.

MASTER SUN
SO THE TASK OF A MILITARY OPERATION IS TO ACCORD DECEPTIVELY WITH THE INTENTIONS OF THE ENEMY. IF YOU CONCENTRATE TOTALLY ON THE ENEMY, YOU CAN KILL ITS MILITARY LEADERSHIP A THOUSAND MILES AWAY. THIS IS SKILLFUL ACCOMPLISHMENT OF THE TASK.

DU MU
If you want to attack an enemy but do not see an opening, then conceal your form and erase your tracks, going along with what the enemy does, not causing any surprises. If the enemy is strong and despises you, you appear to be timid and submissive, going along for the moment with his strength to make him haughty, waiting for him to become complacent and thus vulnerable to attack. If the enemy wants to retreat and go home, you open up a way to let him out, going along with his retreat so that he will not have any desire to fight, ultimately to take advantage of this to attack. Both of these are techniques of according with the enemy.

ZHANG YU
First you go along with their intentions, subsequently you kill their generals—this is skill in accomplishing the task.

MASTER SUN
SO ON THE DAY WAR IS DECLARED, BORDERS ARE CLOSED, PASSPORTS ARE TORN UP, AND EMISSARIES ARE NOT LET THROUGH.

ZHANG YU
Once top-level assessments have been made and military strategy has been developed, then the borders are sealed and passports are revoked, not letting messengers through, lest there be information leaks.

MASTER SUN
MATTERS ARE DEALT WITH STRICTLY AT HEADQUARTERS.

Strictness at headquarters in the planning stage refers to secrecy.

WHEN OPPONENTS PRESENT OPENINGS, YOU SHOULD PENETRATE THEM IMMEDIATELY. GET TO WHAT THEY WANT FIRST, SUBTLY ANTICIPATE THEM. MAINTAIN DISCIPLINE AND ADAPT TO THE ENEMY IN ORDER TO DETERMINE THE OUTCOME OF THE WAR. THUS, AT FIRST YOU ARE LIKE A MAIDEN, SO THE ENEMY OPENS HIS DOOR; THEN YOU ARE LIKE A RABBIT ON THE LOOSE, SO THE ENEMY CANNOT KEEP YOU OUT.

THE NIGHT ATTACK ON THE SANJO PALACE (detail) Kamakura period, 1188–1333
Fenollosa-Weld Collection. Courtesy of the Museum of Fine Arts, Boston

TWELVE

FIRE ATTACK

THERE ARE FIVE KINDS OF FIRE ATTACK: BURNING PEOPLE, BURNING SUPPLIES, BURNING EQUIPMENT, BURNING STOREHOUSES, AND BURNING WEAPONS.

    THE USE OF FIRE MUST HAVE A BASIS, AND REQUIRES CERTAIN TOOLS. THERE ARE APPROPRIATE TIMES FOR SETTING FIRES, NAMELY WHEN THE WEATHER IS DRY AND WINDY.

    GENERALLY, IN FIRE ATTACKS IT IS IMPERATIVE TO FOLLOW UP ON THE CRISES CAUSED BY THE FIRES. WHEN FIRE IS SET INSIDE AN ENEMY CAMP, THEN RESPOND QUICKLY FROM OUTSIDE. IF THE SOLDIERS ARE CALM WHEN FIRE BREAKS OUT, WAIT—DO NOT ATTACK. WHEN THE FIRE REACHES THE HEIGHT OF ITS POWER, FOLLOW UP IF POSSIBLE, HOLD BACK IF NOT.

> MASTER SUN

In general, fire is used to throw enemies into confusion so that you can attack them. It is not simply to destroy enemies with fire. When you hear fire has erupted, you should then attack; once the fire has been brought under control and the people have settled down, it is no use to attack, so Master Sun says you should respond quickly.

> DU MU

WHEN FIRE CAN BE SET OUT IN THE OPEN, DO NOT WAIT UNTIL IT CAN BE SET INSIDE A CAMP—SET IT WHEN THE TIME IS RIGHT.

> MASTER SUN

Fire can also be set outside, in the field; it is not necessary to wait un-

> ZHANG YU

til fire can be set inside an enemy camp. As long as there is an opportunity, fire can be set at an appropriate time.

WHEN FIRE IS SET UPWIND, DO NOT ATTACK DOWNWIND.

MASTER SUN

It is not effective to go against the momentum of the fire, because the enemy will surely fight to the death.

MEI YAOCHEN

IF IT IS WINDY DURING THE DAY, THE WIND WILL STOP AT NIGHT.

MASTER SUN

A daytime wind will stop at night, a night wind will stop at daylight.

MEI YAOCHEN

ARMIES MUST KNOW THERE ARE ADAPTATIONS OF THE FIVE KINDS OF FIRE ATTACK, AND ADHERE TO THEM SCIENTIFICALLY.

MASTER SUN

It will not do just to know how to attack others with fire, it is imperative to know how to prevent others from attacking you. You should figure out the weather patterns and adhere strictly to the principle of setting fire attacks only on suitably windy days.

ZHANG YU

SO THE USE OF FIRE TO HELP AN ATTACK MEANS CLARITY, USE OF WATER TO HELP AT ATTACK MEANS STRENGTH. WATER CAN CUT OFF, BUT CANNOT PLUNDER.

MASTER SUN

When you use fire to help an attack, clearly you can win thereby. Water can be used to divide up an opposing army, so that their force is divided and yours is strong.

ZHANG YU

TO WIN IN BATTLE OR MAKE A SUCCESSFUL SIEGE WITHOUT REWARDING THE MERITORIOUS IS UNLUCKY AND EARNS THE NAME OF STINGINESS. THEREFORE IT IS SAID THAT AN ENLIGHTENED GOVERNMENT CONSIDERS THIS, AND GOOD MILITARY LEADERSHIP REWARDS MERIT. THEY DO NOT MOBILIZE WHEN THERE IS NO ADVANTAGE, DO NOT ACT WHEN THERE IS NOTHING TO GAIN, DO NOT FIGHT WHEN THERE IS NO DANGER.

MASTER SUN

Armaments are instruments of ill omen, war is a dangerous affair. It is imperative to prevent disastrous defeat, so it will not do to mobilize an army for petty reasons—arms are only to be used when there is no choice but to do so.

ZHANG YU

A GOVERNMENT SHOULD NOT MOBILIZE AN ARMY OUT OF ANGER, MILITARY LEADERS SHOULD NOT PROVOKE WAR OUT OF WRATH. ACT WHEN IT IS BENEFICIAL, DESIST IF IT IS NOT. ANGER CAN REVERT TO JOY, WRATH CAN REVERT TO DELIGHT, BUT A NATION DESTROYED CANNOT BE RESTORED TO EXISTENCE, AND THE DEAD CANNOT BE RESTORED TO LIFE. THEREFORE AN ENLIGHTENED GOVERNMENT IS CAREFUL ABOUT THIS, A GOOD MILITARY LEADERSHIP IS ALERT TO THIS. THIS IS THE WAY TO SECURE A NATION AND KEEP THE ARMED FORCES WHOLE.

MASTER SUN

Do not use arms because of your own emotions.

CAO CAO

If you are inconsistent in your feelings, you will lose dignity and trust.

WANG XI

If the government is always prudent about the use of arms, it can thereby make the nation secure. If the military leadership is always wary of taking war lightly, it can therefore keep the armed forces whole.

ZHANG YU

EAGLE
Eighteenth century,
by Ito Jakuchu

THIRTEEN

ON THE USE
OF SPIES

A MAJOR MILITARY OPERATION IS A SEVERE DRAIN ON THE NATION, AND MAY BE KEPT UP FOR YEARS IN THE STRUGGLE FOR ONE DAY'S VICTORY. SO TO FAIL TO KNOW THE CONDITIONS OF OPPONENTS BECAUSE OF RELUCTANCE TO GIVE REWARDS FOR INTELLIGENCE IS EXTREMELY INHUMANE, UNCHARACTERISTIC OF A TRUE MILITARY LEADER, UNCHARACTERISTIC OF AN ASSISTANT OF THE GOVERNMENT, UNCHARACTERISTIC OF A VICTORIOUS CHIEF. SO WHAT ENABLES AN INTELLIGENT GOVERNMENT AND A WISE MILITARY LEADERSHIP TO OVERCOME OTHERS AND ACHIEVE EXTRAORDINARY ACCOMPLISHMENTS IS FOREKNOWLEDGE.

FOREKNOWLEDGE CANNOT BE GOTTEN FROM GHOSTS AND SPIRITS, CANNOT BE HAD BY ANALOGY, CANNOT BE FOUND OUT BY CALCULATION. IT MUST BE OBTAINED FROM PEOPLE, PEOPLE WHO KNOW THE CONDITIONS OF THE ENEMY.

THERE ARE FIVE KINDS OF SPY: THE LOCAL SPY, THE INSIDE SPY, THE REVERSE SPY, THE DEAD SPY, AND THE LIVING SPY. WHEN THE FIVE KINDS OF SPIES ARE ALL ACTIVE, NO ONE KNOWS THEIR ROUTES—THIS IS CALLED ORGANIZATIONAL GENIUS, AND IS VALUABLE TO THE LEADERSHIP.

LOCAL SPIES ARE HIRED FROM AMONG THE PEOPLE OF A LOCALITY. INSIDE SPIES ARE HIRED FROM AMONG ENEMY OFFICIALS. REVERSE SPIES ARE HIRED FROM AMONG ENEMY SPIES. DEAD SPIES TRANSMIT FALSE INTELLIGENCE TO ENEMY SPIES. LIVING SPIES COME BACK TO REPORT.

MASTER SUN

ZHANG YU   Inside spies are drawn from among disaffected officials of the opposing regime, or from among relatives of officials who have been executed.

DU MU   Among officials of the opposing regime, there are intelligent ones who lose their jobs, there are those who are punished for excesses, there are also greedy favorites. There are those confined to the lower ranks, there are those who fail to get appointments, there are those who seek to take advantage of a collapse to extend their own wealth and power, and there are those who always act with deceit and duplicity. Any of them can be secretly approached and bribed so as to find out conditions in their country and discover any plans against you; they can also be used to create rifts and disharmony.

LI QUAN   When enemy agents come to spy on you, bribe them generously to make them spy for you instead. They are then reverse spies, renegades or double agents.

WANG XI   Reverse spies are enemy spies who are detained and induced to give information, or who are sent back with false information. Dead spies are those who are fooled by their own leaders into passing on false information to the enemy; then the facts are determined, they are inevitably killed.

DU YOU   When your spies are given false information that they hand on to the enemy when they are captured, the enemy makes preparations according to this information. When things turn out differently, the spies then die. Therefore they are called dead spies.

DU MU   Living spies are those that come and go with information. For living spies, it is imperative to choose those who are inwardly bright but outwardly appear to be stupid, who are inconspicuous in appearance but strong of heart, who are fast, powerful, and brave, who are immune to seduction, who can endure hunger, cold, and dishonor.

MASTER SUN   THEREFORE NO ONE IN THE ARMED FORCES IS TREATED AS FAMILIARLY AS ARE SPIES, NO ONE IS GIVEN REWARDS AS RICH AS THOSE GIVEN TO SPIES, AND NO MATTER IS MORE SECRET THAN ESPIONAGE.

VIKARALA. Ch'ing dynasty, 1644–1911

DU YOU	If spies are not treated well, they may become renegades and work for the enemy, leaking out information about you. They are given rich rewards and relied upon to do their work. If they do not keep their espionage secret, this is suicidal.
MASTER SUN	ONE CANNOT USE SPIES WITHOUT SAGACITY AND KNOWLEDGE, ONE CANNOT USE SPIES WITHOUT HUMANITY AND JUSTICE, ONE CANNOT GET THE TRUTH FROM SPIES WITHOUT SUBTLETY. THIS IS A VERY DELICATE MATTER INDEED. SPIES ARE USEFUL EVERYWHERE.
DU MU	Every matter requires prior knowledge.
MASTER SUN	IF AN ITEM OF INTELLIGENCE IS HEARD BEFORE A SPY REPORTS IT, THEN BOTH THE SPY AND THE ONE WHO TOLD ABOUT IT DIE.
MEI YAOCHEN	The spy is killed for leaking information, the one who told about it is killed to stop him from talking.
MASTER SUN	WHENEVER YOU WANT TO ATTACK AN ARMY, BESIEGE A CITY, OR KILL A PERSON, FIRST YOU MUST KNOW THE IDENTITIES OF THEIR DEFENDING GENERALS, THEIR ASSOCIATES, THEIR VISITORS, THEIR GATEKEEPERS, AND THEIR CHAMBERLAINS, SO HAVE YOUR SPIES FIND OUT.
DU MU	Whenever you are going to attack and fight, first you have to know the talents of the people employed by the opponent, so you can deal with them according to their abilities.
MASTER SUN	YOU MUST SEEK OUT ENEMY AGENTS WHO HAVE COME TO SPY ON YOU, BRIBE THEM AND INDUCE THEM TO STAY WITH YOU, SO YOU CAN USE THEM AS REVERSE SPIES. BY INTELLIGENCE THUS OBTAINED, YOU CAN FIND LOCAL SPIES AND INSIDE SPIES TO EMPLOY. BY INTELLIGENCE THUS OBTAINED, YOU CAN CAUSE THE MISINFORMATION OF DEAD SPIES TO BE CONVEYED TO THE ENEMY. BY INTELLIGENCE THUS OBTAINED, YOU CAN GET LIVING SPIES TO WORK AS PLANNED.
ZHANG YU	By means of these reverse spies, you find out greedy locals and vulnerable officials who can be induced to work for you. By means of these

reverse spies, you can find out how the enemy can be deceived, and send dead spies to misinform them. By means of these reverse spies you can find out the conditions of the enemy, so that living spies can go and return as planned.

IT IS ESSENTIAL FOR A LEADER TO KNOW ABOUT THE FIVE KINDS OF ESPIONAGE, AND THIS KNOWLEDGE DEPENDS ON REVERSE SPIES, SO REVERSE SPIES MUST BE TREATED WELL.

MASTER SUN

It is by finding out the conditions of the enemy through the agency of reverse spies that all the other kinds of espionage can be used, so reverse spies, renegades or double agents, are most important and must be treated well.

DU MU

SO ONLY A BRILLIANT RULER OR A WISE GENERAL WHO CAN USE THE HIGHLY INTELLIGENT FOR ESPIONAGE IS SURE OF GREAT SUCCESS. THIS IS ESSENTIAL FOR MILITARY OPERATIONS, AND THE ARMIES DEPEND ON THIS IN THEIR ACTIONS.

MASTER SUN

It will not do for the army to act without knowing the opponent's condition, and to know the opponent's condition is impossible without espionage.

DU MU

CREDITS